POPULISM AND THE EUROPEAN CULTURE WARS

Concern and hostility towards populism has become a distinctive feature of contemporary political culture. In Europe such concerns are frequently directed at Eurosceptics, whose opposition to the European Union is often portrayed as a cultural crime. Ancient anti-democratic claims about the gullibility, ignorance and irrationality of the masses are frequently recycled through the anti-populist condemnation of people who vote the wrong way.

This book argues that the current outburst of anti-populist anxiety is symptomatic of a loss of faith in democracy and in the ability of the *demos* to assume the role of responsible citizens. Distrust of the people and of parliamentary sovereignty is reinforced by the concern that, on its own, liberal democracy lacks the normative foundation to inspire the loyalty and affection of ordinary citizens. By focusing on the conflict between the European Union's Commission and the Government of Hungary, this book explores contrasting attitudes towards national sovereignty, popular sovereignty, the question of tradition, and the past that are the main drivers of the Culture War in Europe.

Frank Furedi is Emeritus Professor of Sociology, University of Kent, UK.

POPULISM AND THE EUROPEAN CULTURE WARS

The Conflict of Values Between Hungary and the EU

Frank Furedi

Routledge
Taylor & Francis Group

LONDON AND NEW YORK

First published 2018
by Routledge
2 Park Square, Milton Park, Abingdon, Oxon OX14 4RN

and by Routledge
711 Third Avenue, New York, NY 10017

Routledge is an imprint of the Taylor & Francis Group, an informa business

British Library Cataloguing-in-Publication Data
A catalogue record for this book is available from the British Library

Library of Congress Cataloging-in-Publication Data
A catalog record for this book has been requested

ISBN: 978-1-138-09740-7 (hbk)
ISBN: 978-1-138-09743-8 (pbk)
ISBN: 978-1-315-10489-8 (ebk)

Typeset in Bembo
by Apex CoVantage, LLC

CONTENTS

PREFACE

In recent years I have become concerned about the development of an anti-populist cultural *zeitgeist* in Western societies. Such sentiments are particularly influential within the media and cultural and educational establishments. These institutions have adopted the habit of applying the populist label to movements and groups whose values contradict their own. Populism is not used as a neutral term of description: it conveys the connotation of moral inferiority. Narratives about populism also often suggest that these movements are dangerous, extreme, and a threat to a democratic society.

In Europe the anti-populist narrative is frequently directed at Eurosceptics, whose opposition to the European Union (EU) is often portrayed as a cultural crime. Old oligarchical claims about the gullibility, ignorance, and irrationality of the masses, which were originally formulated in Ancient Greece, are frequently recycled through the anti-populist condemnation of people who vote 'the wrong way'. During my discussions with educated supporters of the EU, I have often found myself having to defend citizens who voted for Brexit from the charge of racism or fascism.

Disappointment with the capacity of the people to vote the right way has led to the publication of a spate of anti-populist literature that questions the value of democracy itself.[1] Such sentiments gained considerable force after Britain's vote for Brexit and especially after the election of Donald Trump as President of the United States. That so many commentators appeared to be so selective about their commitment to democracy indicates that one of the most fundamental values of an enlightened and open society is the danger of losing its moral authority. So although the media's attention is focused on the supposed threat posed by populist movements, I have drawn the conclusion that the anti-populist reaction to them, represents a far greater menace to democratic politics.

My concern about the anti-populist turn of Western elite culture was reinforced by the way that my country of birth – Hungary – has been portrayed in the media.

Hungary has become one of the favourite targets of anti-populist currents in Western Europe. To try to make sense of the tensions that have erupted between the leaders of the EU – particularly the European Commission – and the Hungarian government, I undertook a study of the key issues at stake in this dispute. As I explain in this book, these tensions are the international reflection of the cultural conflicts that often occur within the domestic sphere between populist and anti-populist interests.

I have found this book a difficult one to write. Despite my attachment to the political values of popular sovereignty, secular humanism, freedom of speech, and freedom of movement, I have found myself defending a nationalist, Christian conservative government from criticisms that I consider to be manifestly unfair. Though many of Hungary's critics perceive themselves as 'liberal', their anti-populist sentiments are characteristically illiberal and disturbingly intolerant. They often come across as latter-day cultural imperialists who feel that they have the right to impose their values on Hungarian society and who have no inhibitions about lecturing Hungarians on how to live their lives. They do not seem to realize that the problems facing Hungarian society will be only resolved through the efforts of its people, not by foreign advocacy organizations meddling in the affairs of an independent sovereign nation.

During my stay in Budapest it became evident to me that many Hungarians do not understand why their political culture is condemned with such hostility by sections of the Western media. They are often surprised to discover that what they perceive as their 'old-fashioned' ways are sometimes regarded as anathema by foreign observers. I hope this book helps them to gain insight into the dynamics of what is, in many ways, a confusing conflict over the values that give meaning to people's lives. At the same time I hope that my Western readers will find this book useful for gaining an insight into the cultural values that motivate the behaviour of their Eastern neighbours. Cultural tensions between West and East Europe refract conflicts that also lie deep within Western societies.

The current Culture War against populism is often focused around different conceptions of history: the meaning of the past and its relevance for today. While in Budapest, I enjoyed the hospitality of the Institution for the Research on Eastern and Central European History and Society. The head of this institute, the eminent Hungarian historian Dr Mária Schmidt, strongly supported my attempt to formulate my ideas about the politics of memory in the Hungarian context.

A grant from the Arthur Koestler Research Programme greatly assisted the research that I carried out for this book. I am grateful to the institute's archivist Orsolya Büki for directing me towards important Hungarian sources that helped me clarify my confusions. Dr Vanessa Pupavac of Nottingham University helped me understand how the European Commission's attitude towards Hungary is paralleled by its imperious behaviour in the Balkans.

Note

1 See for example Brenan, J. (2016) *Against Democracy*, Princeton University Press: Princeton.

INTRODUCTION

In recent years I have become interested in, and concerned about, the growing tendency to invoke the word 'populism' as a shorthand for morally condemning a significant section of the European electorate. Mainstream politicians and commentators invariably use the term to convey the idea that they are referring to people who are irrational, uneducated, likely to be Eurosceptic, and nationalist. According to this caricature, they are emotionally prejudiced and probably racist and xenophobic, if not borderline fascists. Other qualities associated with the populist mindset are a disposition towards religiosity, nationalism, traditionalism, and conventional 'out of date' lifestyles. In the language of their post-modern, post-traditional, and post-national critics, they are not 'aware', 'emotionally literate', or 'cosmopolitan'. Leaders of the EU, such as Jean-Claude Juncker, the President of the European Commission (EC), appear to believe that the fight against populism is akin to an obligation to wage a holy war. When Juncker declares that 'we have to fight nationalism' and 'block the avenue of populism', he frequently evokes memories associated with the good fight against fascism.[1]

The pathology of populism is not only diagnosed as an individual malady or defect, but also as one that afflicts communities and nations. In recent years, Hungary has sometimes been depicted as a pariah nation, whose government promotes the worst form of extreme populism. Anyone perusing the European press would quickly gain the impression that Hungary is in the throes of an authoritarian populist revolution. Advocates of European federalism continually lecture Hungarians for allegedly violating European values and for showing a flagrant disrespect for democracy. One British journalist writing in the *Financial Times* claims that, given its numerous misdeeds and xenophobic behaviour, if Hungary applied to join the EU today it would not be granted membership. The journalist noted that, 'since taking power in 2010, Prime Minister Orbán has compromised judicial independence and restricted media freedom while openly declaring his intention to emulate the authoritarian practices of states like Russia and China.'[2]

At times, criticism of Hungary is directed not simply at its government, but at an ungrateful people who appear to be incorrigibly nationalistic and racist. During the European migration crisis, the entire Hungarian nation came under scrutiny for its government's refusal to open its borders to the flow of migrants. Reading about this issue in the Western press, it was difficult to be sure whether they were recycling stories about the horrors of the Nazi era or describing events today. Robert Fisk, a correspondent for *The Independent*, likened the Hungarian authorities' policing of crowds of migrants to Nazis shepherding their victims onto a train to Auschwitz. He noted:

> Funny how the old memory buds don't kick in at this point. For just 71 years ago, the Hungarian police were forcing tens of thousands of Jews on to trains out of Budapest, desperate to get them to Auschwitz on time. Adolf Eichmann was setting the rules.[3]

The sudden and unexpected reappearance of Adolf Eichmann on the streets of twenty-first-century Budapest is an increasingly acceptable rhetorical flourish in the crusade against populism. What is particularly disturbing about Fisk's polemic against Hungary is its demonization of the entire Hungarian people. 'And don't think that Hungarians were unwilling tools of Germany's march into Hungary towards the end of the war.' he wrote, just in case you missed his point.

At times, Fisk appears as a modern-day personification of Kurtz in Joseph Conrad's novel, *Heart of Darkness*. At the start of Conrad's novel, Kurtz believes he can help primitive Africans to see the light and become civilized. However, he soon abandons this project and sees only depravity and darkness. Perhaps a few years ago, Fisk also believed that the much-damaged and, in his words, 'politically unreconstructed' nations of Eastern Europe could be educated to become worthy members of the EU. He laments that, 'I always thought we were a bit too quick to open our arms to them.' But now 'we are beginning to discover what the Hungarian state looks like' – that is, we see the heart of darkness that is Hungary. Without a hint of irony, this journalist condemns Hungarians for their racism, and in doing so, fails to reflect on how he himself dehumanizes this people.

In all likelihood, Kurtz really believed what he saw – and I have no reason to doubt the integrity of critics of Hungary's populism. Many of them genuinely regard supporters of what they call 'populist movements' as, at best, deluded and miseducated, and at worst anti-immigrant and racist. In my discussions with supporters of European federalism, I have become convinced that they sincerely believe that Hungary no longer has a free press, that its democracy is a sham, and that basic freedoms are under threat.

One of the reasons why I wrote *Populism and the Culture Wars in Europe* was to reflect on how a clash of values has led to a polarized perception of reality. The politicization of culture contains the potential for expressing conflicts and problems in a form that is difficult to resolve. As the sociologist Donald Black explains, 'culture is a zero-sum game', and for that reason can rarely be resolved through a compromise.[4]

It often appears that cultural conflicts provoke far more visceral reactions than those produced by ideological disputes. Ideological differences on issues, such as the role of the welfare state or the free market, may be partially mediated through pragmatism and compromise. Values dominating cultural conflicts over issues like abortion, gay marriage, multiculturalism, national sovereignty – to name a few – are often far less susceptible to compromise than differences on social and economic matters. Conflicts over values touch on moral issues to do with good and evil, and in such conditions, the different parties of a debate are all too ready to ascribe the worst possible motives to one another.

In such circumstances, empathy is in short supply and the protagonists are far too ready to resort to the language of evil to describe each other. In this respect, the current Culture Wars over values resembles the religious wars that afflicted Europe in the early modern era. My main interest in writing this book is to explore those dimensions of the Culture Wars that help clarify the tension in Europe between the EU and populism. One reason why I focus on Hungary is because it is often cited as the heartland of the populist phenomenon and has been at the centre of this conflict in Europe. In numerous polemics directed at populism, Hungary is depicted as the most extreme example of this political movement. For example, the journalist Jean Quatremer of the newspaper *Liberation* recently warned that Viktor Orbán's populist model is 'taking hold across the whole of Europe'.[5] Exploring the tension between the Western anti-populist worldview and what Quatremer called Hungary's 'populist model' provides a useful way of analysing the dynamic driving the conflict of values that appears to dominate so much of public life.

My interest in writing this book was first provoked by the desire to understand why Hungary has become the subject of so much international condemnation. As someone born in Hungary but raised in the West, I felt that I should use my sociological training to interpret possible acts of miscommunication between the two sides. I was particularly puzzled by the evident double standard that is often expressed through the criticisms of Hungary made by foreign observers. For example, British journalists who condemned Hungary for refusing to allow migrants to enter their country rarely observed that there were very real parallels with the stand taken by their own government's attitude towards migrants in Calais. Similarly, media reports highlighted the iniquity of Hungary building a fence on the border separating it from Serbia in order to stop the flow of migrants into the country. However, the reaction of the media was very different when Norway built a fence on the border with Russia to keep migrants out. The Western media's reaction to the Baltic states – Estonia, Latvia, and Lithuania – building a 250-mile fence along their eastern frontier was also strikingly different to their commentary on the Hungarian fence. The fence-building activities of these nations were judged according to a very different moral standard.

The application of this double standard was particularly striking in relation to the introduction of a series of laws in Hungary, in early January 2011, which were designed to increase the state's control of the media. The introduction of this law led to the eruption of widespread indignation and criticism by EU leaders and foreign politicians. The then President of the EU Commission, José Manuel Barroso, stated that the 'freedom of the press is a sacred principle' and warned that he would take up the matter with the Hungarian prime minister. Numerous non-governmental organizations (NGOs) and international bodies also condemned the new law. The Organisation for Security and Co-operation in Europe (OSCE) stated that the law 'endangers editorial independence and media pluralism'.[6]

Speaking on the day that Hungary began its six-month presidency of the EU, Orbán fought back against his foreign critics. He accused them of practising a double standard, arguing: 'I defy anyone to find anything in our law that is not in other EU member states' media laws.' He indicated that he would be prepared to accept the EU's ruling on the legality of the law, but also said that if Hungary's legislation had to be changed, 'so too would similar laws in France, Germany and the Netherlands'.

As a liberal free speech campaigner, I oppose the imposition of any form of censorship and the introduction of legal instruments to control and regulate the media, whether in Hungary or England. But while I regret the introduction of Hungary's media law, Orbán had a point when he claimed that this law is not radically different from those in other parts of the EU. In recent years, freedom of speech in Europe has been compromised by a series of laws seeking to censor 'hate speech', speech likely to cause distress, Holocaust denial, and 'incitement to violence'. The Leveson Inquiry in the United Kingdom, leading to the expansion of press regulation, indicates that Hungary certainly does not have a monopoly on illiberal media laws.

The European Convention on Human Rights (ECHR) significantly qualifies the claim that the EU regards the freedom of speech and of the press as a 'sacred principle'. It states that 'everyone has the right to freedom of expression' without state interference, but then imposes important conditions on the exercise of this right. The ECHR notes:

> The exercise of these freedoms, since it carries with it duties and responsibilities, may be subject to such formalities, conditions, restrictions or penalties as are prescribed by law and are necessary in a democratic society, in the interests of national security, territorial integrity or public safety, for the prevention of disorder or crime, for the protection of health or morals, for the protection of the reputation or rights of others, for preventing the disclosure of information received in confidence, or for maintaining the authority and impartiality of the judiciary.

Many of these potential 'conditions and restrictions', such as 'the protection of health or morals', are not unlike the moral restraints imposed on the media by the Hungarian law. As one fierce critic of the Orbán regime acknowledges, 'it is largely the EU's left-liberal political elites who have opened the door for Fidesz on the issue by introducing legislation that limits a free press and free speech in other countries.' Peter Wilkin, despite his hostility to what he characterizes as Hungary's

'Road to Serfdom', concedes that the Hungarian government's claim that 'they are merely following EU-wide norms' is 'defensible'.[7]

Critics have also objected to the establishment of a highly centralized media authority that is charged with overseeing and regulating all public and news production outlets. The launching of a state-run media surveillance authority, composed of political appointees, provided a powerful instrument for the control of the media. However, Hungary is not the only EU member state where employees of media supervisory authorities are government appointees. Austria, Sweden, the Netherlands, Ireland, and Denmark all have political appointees on their media regulatory bodies.

The enactment of Hungary's new constitution, known as the New Hungarian Fundamental Law, which came into force in January 2012, was condemned as a uniquely anti-democratic law that violated the elementary norm of separating religion and state. The new constitution came under fire for its explicit affirmation of Christian values, which, it claims, are historically essential for the preservation of the Hungarian nation. Anyone reviewing the objections made by international critics of Hungary's allegedly anti-democratic and Christian constitution could be forgiven for concluding that religion is absent from the foundational laws of other European societies. Yet the Constitutions of numerous European countries, including Greece, Bulgaria, and Ireland, make explicit references to their Christian faith. The Constitution of Malta boldly declares that Catholicism is its state religion, and the Danish Constitution notes that the Evangelical Lutheran Church is the Established Church of Denmark. Although Norway is a secular society, the Church of Norway is mentioned in its Constitution; the United Kingdom has an unwritten Constitution that places the head of the state at the helm of the Anglican Church. It is worth mentioning in passing that despite all the fuss about its Christian Constitution, Hungary, unlike some European nations, does not have a state or official religion.

Hungary's Fundamental Law does affirm values that are traditional and conservative. It is also explicitly illiberal. However, contrary to the view expressed by many of its international critics, it is not anti-democratic. As the American political scientist Laura Ymayo Tartakoff explained, 'the new Constitution did not fundamentally change the existing structure of government. Hungary remains a unicameral parliamentary republic, based on separation of powers and the protection of fundamental rights.'[8]

Critics of the Fundamental Law rarely acknowledge that it is the first Hungarian Constitution to be enacted within a parliamentary framework after a free election. It is a constitution enacted by a government with an overwhelming democratic mandate. Moreover, the Western media simply overlooked the fact that the pre-Orbán Constitution of Hungary lacked any democratic mandate: it was enacted on 20 August 1949 as part of the consolidation of the Moscow-dominated Stalinist regime in Hungary. Opponents of the Fundamental Law did not think it odd that an undemocratically-enacted Constitution imposed on Hungary by a former superpower should be considered morally superior to one based on a democratic mandate.

Problem of language

In the course of researching and writing this book, I often found reliance on the conventional political vocabulary more of a hindrance than a help. Consequently, I have become convinced that far more attention needs to be paid to concepts such as 'left' and 'right', 'neoliberal', 'liberal', 'political correctness', and 'populist'. In the specific context of the European Culture Wars, these concepts do little to clarify the issues at stake.

In the setting of Hungary, political debate is often described as a clash between the right-wing populist government of Viktor Orbán's Fidesz and his 'leftist' and 'liberal' opponents. Whatever these labels mean, they have little in common with the classical usage of these terms. The political outlook of Fidesz is best described as a synthesis of conservative nationalism and Christian democracy. Insofar as it seeks to address the people of Hungary, its politics contain an important plebeian dimension. However, it does not share the hostility and suspicion that classical populism directs towards elites. Fidesz criticizes neoliberal and EU elites. But as one of Fidesz's academic critics concedes, 'even in its most populist phase the party refrained from condemning the entire elite and elements of elitist conservatism have never completely disappeared from the party's discourse'.[9] Within the Hungarian vernacular, Fidesz is best described as a *polgári* party. In Hungarian, the word *polgári* encompasses civil, citizen, and bourgeois; it is the middle-class *bourgeois-citizen* that constitutes the imagined audience for Fidesz.

One possible reason why foreign critics of Hungary fail to characterize the politics of the government accurately is that they rarely encounter traditional conservatives in their own societies. Many parties that are associated with conservatism in Western Europe, such as the British Tories or the German Christian Democrats, have become estranged from the traditional values of their movement. In the 1970s, they self-consciously promoted traditional conservative values and frequently argued for going 'back to basics': upholding the traditional family and affirming religious morality and loyalty to nation. However, they found it difficult to promote these conservative values and win support for them. As a result of the setbacks suffered in the Culture Wars of the 1960s, West European conservatives went on the defensive and became hesitant about arguing for traditional values.[10] Since that time, periodic attempts to relaunch the conservative project often concluded with the plea to get rid of the old ideological baggage and to modernize.

In contrast to Western conservatives, Hungary's Fidesz government is unapologetically traditional. Its celebration of religion, the traditional family, and patriotism echoes the narrative that European conservative parties actively promoted as late as the 1970s. Whereas in Western Europe conservatives are reluctant to call themselves right wing, their Eastern European counterparts have no inhibitions on this score.

The application of the terms left and liberal to capture the outlook of the Hungarian opposition is even more confusing. Since the regime change – the transition from the Soviet client regime in Hungary to an independent sovereign nation – during 1989–1990, parties described as liberal or left wing have adopted policies and practices that, in the British context, could be described as a synthesis of Thatcherite and Blairite politics. Almost overnight, members of the previous governing Communist Party re-emerged as unapologetic free-marketeers. Socialist politicians and governments were at the forefront of introducing an economic shock therapy that led to the privatization of the economy, mass unemployment, and the dismantling of the old Hungarian welfare state. The defining feature of those who are described, or self-identify, as liberals in Hungary is their uncritical internalization of the technocratic and elitist worldview of mainstream EU politics. They are no less intolerant than their political opponents. So when they were in government, they were as devoted to managing the media as the regimes that followed them.

The socialist government before the election of Fidesz in 2010, was a regime devoted to the practice of technocratic governance. Technocratic governance eschews classical political principles and seeks to legitimate itself on the basis of expertise and process. With the exception of the EU, technocratic governance rarely exists in a pure form. The EU has always suffered from a democratic deficit, and its claim to legitimacy has relied on its claim to expert authority. On its own, technocratic governance lacks the capacity to motivate and inspire. It therefore relies on policies and ideals that are external to itself to retain credibility. From the tradition of the old right, technocratic governance has adopted market-oriented economics with its promise of future prosperity to justify its socio-economic programme. From the cultural left, it has internalized the ethos of anti-national, minority identity politics. During the first two decades following regime change in Budapest, the EU's free market policies, which ran in parallel with its minority identity politics, became assimilated by Hungarian parties who described themselves as left or liberal.

The usage of the term 'populism' to explain contemporary issues is especially devoid of conceptual clarity. In our time, populism is a term that anti-populists use to describe people they do not like. I have yet to come across a card-carrying populist in any part of Europe, and when I ask people in Budapest about their populism they look bemused. One history undergraduate student explained to me that when 'you guys in the West call us populist, what you really mean is that we are a bunch of provincial hicks'.

The meaning of twenty-first-century populism is fraught with difficulty because its usage has been so heavily influenced by the anti-populist temper that dominates public language. In previous times, populism served as a form of self-designation, and people knowingly described themselves using this term. During the nineteenth century, the Narodniks in Russia, like the People's Party in the United States took pride in their populist outlook. In the twenty-first century, however, it is the advocates of anti-populism who define their opponents as populist. The political scientist Ivan Krastev raised an important question when he asked 'who decides which policies are "populist" and which are "sound"?'[11] In the contemporary era, this decision has become the prerogative of a coterie of influential anti-populists.

In the twenty-first century, the meaning of populism has been distorted through the tendency of its opponents to attribute a wide range of negative qualities to it. The academic literature on populism is typically hostile to its subject matter and often projects values and attitudes on movements that its members would not recognize as their own. For example, a book on *The Politics of Fear* associates populist 'EU-scepticism' with a 'chauvinist, nativist view of "the people" and with an extreme right wing orientation.'[12] While this coupling of extreme right-wing inclinations with Euroscepticism is no doubt an outcome of a genuine incomprehension of the phenomenon, it also distorts a reality where the aspiration for democracy and solidarity has disillusioned millions of people within the EU.

The mainstream academic literature on populism is characteristically anti-populist and, in some cases, tends to treat its subject matter with the kind of hostility that is usually directed at an enemy. For example, Abts and Rummens argue that the logic of populism violates 'the symbolic framework that defines the political stage for democratic political struggles', and they are 'no longer ordinary adversaries, but *political enemies* who hold an incompatible view of the symbolic structure of the locus of power itself'. They add 'that it is important that populist parties, to the extent that they are inimical to democracy, should be revealed as such, treated accordingly and, if necessary, isolated from power'.[13] This representation of populism as an enemy that needs to be isolated explicitly seeks to quarantine society from its pernicious doctrines.

The tendency to pathologize populism is contested by a minority of scholars. Cristóbal Rovira Kaltwasser has noted that 'many authors maintain that populism is first and foremost a democratic disease or pathology'.[14] Ernesto Laclau's study, *On Populist Reason*, notes how the use of this concept has become integral to the denigration of the masses. He wrote that central to the 'strategies of the anti-populist onslaught' is the attempt to render it abnormal and the construction of 'an ascetic political universe from which its dangerous logics had to be excluded'.[15]

However, what even critics of the demonization of populism rarely explore is the spectacular growth of the influence of a stand-alone anti-populist cultural script in recent decades. Hostility towards the *demos* has at every stage accompanied the historical emergence of democracy. The rise of mass politics since the nineteenth century has continually provoked the fear and hostility of the political establishment. These old concerns have gained a new form in recent times as a result of the cultural conflicts that dominate public life in Western societies. In the current context of the twenty-first century's Culture Wars, anti-populism is particularly hostile to the values that it attributes to its populist opponents.

One of the objectives of *Populism and the Culture Wars in Europe* is to explore the phenomenon of anti-populism – a powerful narrative that dominates the media landscape in Western societies. Anti-populism has constructed a culturally warped view of populism that casts a movement questioning the elite cultural consensus in a negative light. According to this cultural script, populist movements are xenophobic, anti-democratic, and potentially threaten to bring back the totalitarian era of the 1930s. The continual framing of populism as a budding-totalitarian movement that threatens to bring back the bad old days has become a recurrent theme in the Western media. Even religious figures have internalized the anti-populist cultural script. Pope Francis has not yet issued a papal bull against populism, but he has warned that populism could lead to the election of 'saviours' who are similar to Hitler. He also echoed the anti-populist script when he stated, 'the example of populism in the European sense of the word is Germany in 1933'. Here, the Pope did not merely compare today with the past and use the phrase '*like* 1933' – he went a step further and said populism '*is* Germany in 1933'.[16] When Pope Francis asserts that 'populism is evil', it becomes evident that the anti-populist cultural script possesses a highly charged moralistic character.[17]

As the British sociologist Jennie Bristow has noted, sociology developed the concept of a cultural script to better understand how 'culture is used' in 'framing how phenomena are understood'.[18] Hopefully this study will help clarify how the anti-populist cultural script fails to grasp the phenomenon that its purports to represent. As someone committed to the principle of popular sovereignty and freedom, what I offer is a radical democratic reading of the conflict of values prevailing in Europe. My aim is to explore what I take to be the key themes in the cultural conflict between the sides. Through my focus on the Hungarian question, I hope to illuminate the wider underlying patterns that shape the conflict of values throughout the EU. As I try to explain, contrasting attitudes towards national sovereignty, popular sovereignty, and the questions of tradition and the past are the main drivers of the Culture Wars in Europe.

One final point. Given the confusion that surrounds the usage of the term populist, I use the term with hesitation. The *Oxford English Dictionary* defines populism as 'the policies or principles of any of various political parties which seek to represent the interests of ordinary people'. Though very general and ahistorical, this definition captures an important dimension of the populist impulse. The attempt to 'represent the interests of ordinary people' characterizes the stated aims of a wide variety of movements, who are often politically hostile to one another. In the current era, what distinguishes different movements labelled as populist is their rejection of Western elite culture and values. Despite the attempt to represent populist movements as a distinct political species, they have little in common, other than their hostility to the ideals and the political practices of the holders of power. Insofar as there is a common goal that distinguishes the Brexit voter and the supporter of Podemos from the parties of the oligarchy, it is an aspiration for solidarity and for community. So insofar as populism has a real existence, it reflects this aspiration rather than a distinct political outlook.

Notes

1 Cited in Savage, M. (2016) 'Borders Are Worst Invention Ever, Declares Juncker', *The Times*, 23 August 2016.
2 Clark, D. (2016) 'Europe's Obsession with the Past Risks Blinding It to the Dangers of the Present', *FT blog*, 4 May 2016, http://blogs.ft.com/beyond-brics/2016/03/04/europes-obsession-with-the-past-risks-blinding-it-to-the-dangers-of-the-present/.
3 www.independent.co.uk/voices/comment/hungary-must-look-to-its-own-history-for-migrant-guidance-10488880.html.
4 Black (2011) p. s101.

5 www.euronews.com/2016/01/06/hungary-s-populist-model-is-taking-hold-across-the-whole-of-europe-says-analyst.
6 See www.reuters.com/article/us-hungary-media-insight-idUSBREA1I08C20140219.
7 See Wilkin (2016) pp. 126, 127.
8 Tartakoff (2012) p. 360.
9 Enyedi (2015) p. 234.
10 I discuss the defeat of conservative values in the Culture War in Furedi (2014) Chapter 6.
11 Krastev (2007)
12 See Wodak (2015) pp. 41–43 & 54–55.
13 See Abts & Rummens (2007) pp. 423–424.
14 Kaltwasser (2014) p. 470.
15 Laclau (2007) p. 19.
16 www.washingtonpost.com/news/worldviews/wp/2017/02/17/in-a-new-letter-pope-francis-tells-activists-to-stand-up-to-populists/?utm_term=.2504bd3be112.
17 See www.independent.co.uk/news/world/americas/pope-francis-warning-donald-trump-populism-evil-die-zelt-ends-badly-western-democracy-a7620016.html.
18 See Bristow (2015) p. 13.

1

WHO DECIDES EUROPE'S VALUES?

Throughout the Western world, values have become a focus of conflict. Societies find it difficult to establish a consensus on moral norms. Indeed the passions that were once devoted to settling ideological differences are today directed towards engaging in a conflict over values. During the recent decades, all the major conflicts in society have in one way or another been linked to disputes over cultural values. These so-called *Culture Wars* first emerged in the United States in the 1960s. Acrimonious arguments about family life, the role of religion, sexuality, marriage, the end of life, and abortion indicate that there is little consensus on the fundamental values that guide human behaviour in American society. Conflicting attitudes towards cultural values escalated into a veritable war during the 2016 US presidential elections.

In recent times, the Culture Wars have also made their presence felt on the landscape of Europe. Here, controversy has focused on the role of religion, particularly Christianity and, lately, Islam; on the meaning of European culture; on multiculturalism; and on the value of national sentiment. The key issue that underlies all these different controversies is a conflict over the status of national sovereignty and the nation state. The transnational outlook that pervades the institutions of the EU regards national sovereignty as an outdated and potentially disruptive ideal. Such differences over values exist both within member states of the EU and across national boundaries, where they roughly correspond to the old division between East and West Europe.

That the Culture Wars have migrated across the Atlantic was vividly demonstrated during a debate in the European Parliament in January 2012. The debate, titled 'Recent Political Developments in Hungary',[1] was organized as a response to concerns expressed by the EC that a variety of recently enacted Hungarian laws violated the values of the EU. The commission followed up its concerns by launching infringement proceedings against Hungary on three matters: the independence of the national central bank, the retirement age of judges, and the independence of the data protection authority. Outwardly at least, this controversy appeared as a dispute about relatively routine technical matters; but as the debate unfolded, it became evident that what motivated the main protagonists were different visions of values.

Before the scheduling of this debate, EU-phile commentators in the media and policymakers had singled out the Hungarian government and its recently enacted Constitution, the 'Fundamental Law', as representing a challenge to the secular, democratic, and liberal values of the EU. Frequently, this Constitution's references to Hungary's national and Christian traditions were portrayed as dangerous sentiments that threatened to unleash the resurgence of the xenophobic nationalism the EU believed it had left behind in the 1940s.

José Manuel Barroso, the then president of the EC, set the tone when he introduced the debate. He characterized his differences with the actions of the Hungarian government as an 'extremely sensitive matter, where I believe we have to be clear on values'. Barroso did not clarify what values were at stake, and he was anything but clear on this issue. However, the implication of his statement was that the Hungarian laws and Constitution violated European values.

Hungary's prime minister, Viktor Orbán, responded to Barroso by insisting that the new Constitution and the subsequent measures enacted by his government 'took place on the basis of European values and principles'. He went out of his way to reiterate his government's adherence to European values and concluded his remarks with the words, 'I ask you to continue to support in the future, in the spirit of European values, the major transformation and restructuring that we are in the process of completing in Hungary.'[2] Implicit in his statement was the view that there was more than one version of the meaning of European values, and that respecting the right of different nations to interpret them in line with their own traditions was one of them.

During the course of the debate that followed the initial remarks, it became evident that, despite a common rhetorical affirmation of European values, there was a fundamental difference in the way they were interpreted. Speaker after speaker condemned the Hungarian government for its supposed violation of European values. The Flemish Belgian politician, Guy Verhofstadt, leader of the Group of the Alliance of Liberals and Democrats for Europe, took the floor to denounce the Hungarian government's alleged violation of European values. He warned that what was at issue in the debate were not trivial technical issues but the fundamental principles on which the EU was constructed. He stated:

> What is necessary here is not a debate on technical issues, as we had at the beginning of the year. This is about checking the conformity of the [Hungarian] constitution and cardinal laws with the European values that are enshrined in Article 2 of the Treaty: democracy, the rule of law, freedom of religion, freedom of expression and so on.

Verhofstadt demanded that the EU's Committee on Civil Rights, Justice and Home Affairs draw up a report investigating the actions of the Hungarian government to find out whether 'there exists a clear risk or a serious breach of our values'. His use of the term 'our values' conveyed the implication that they were likely to be different than 'theirs'.

The oddity of the demand that a member state of the EU – a sovereign nation – should have its values policed was left unremarked. What this call for value – policing suggested was that the EU's highly acclaimed celebration of the principle of diversity did not apply to different orientations to values and moral norms across national boundaries. Tolerance for the diversity of values – which has been historically a central feature of liberal thought – was clearly not seen as important by those calling for the monitoring of values in Hungary.

Some of the criticisms directed against Orbán were couched in a language that was less restrained than the legalistic jargon used by Verhofstadt. Daniel Cohn-Bendit of the Greens-European Free Alliance condemned the direction taken by Hungary and lectured Orbán that 'we are here to tell you that you are going in the direction of Hugo Chavez, Fidel Castro, and all the other totalitarian authoritarian governments'. Orbán's response to the charge that Hungary was travelling down a totalitarian route was to declare that his values were no less European than those of his detractors.

From Orbán's perspective, the traditionalist system of values promoted by his government were rooted in the historical legacy of European cultural norms. He argued that:

> Our ideals are undoubtedly Christian and based on personal responsibility; we find national sentiment to be an important and positive thing, and we believe that families are the foundations of the future. It may be that a great many people believe otherwise, but that makes our position no less a European one. It may be that with this we are in a minority in Europe, but this position is no less a European position, and we are free to represent this conviction.

In defence of his argument, Orbán pointed to the former French foreign minister Robert Schuman, considered to be one of the founding fathers of the EU, who stated 'there will either be a Christian democracy in Europe or there will be no democracy at all'.

What was significant about Orbán's response to the criticism levelled against his government was the emphasis that he attached to the politics of culture. 'We Hungarians believe that what makes Europe Europe is its culture', he stated. The implication of Orbán's statement was that his government stood for a system of cultural norms that, though they contradicted the values of his opponents, were rooted in Europe's historical tradition.

Orbán's affirmation of traditional Christian values provoked respondents to claim that his approach violated the spirit of the modern values of pluralism and diversity. Verhofstadt indicated that the Hungarian Constitution was antithetical to European values such as 'democracy, the rule of law, the freedom of religion, the freedom of expression, equality also'. Some of Orbán's critics went a step further and insisted that Christianity was entirely alien to the values of the EU. Taking this sceptical approach to religion, the French Member of the European Parliament (MEP), Marie-Christine Vergiat, representing the Left Bloc, asserted that 'European values are not Christian values'. She claimed that 'European values are freedom of conscience, freedom to believe in a religion of one's choice, freedom to believe or not believe'.

Vergiat's disassociation of European values from Christianity expresses the political sentiment that is integral to the outlook of the secular liberal and leftist post-war tradition. However, it should be noted that this outlook has never monopolized the prevailing definition of European values, and it certainly runs counter to the way it was perceived by the advocates of European integration in the past. Schuman, who is proclaimed as one of the 'Founding Fathers' of European integration, was in no doubt about the foundational role of Christianity for this project. In 1958 he proclaimed that, 'we are called to bethink ourselves of the Christian basics of Europe by forming a democratic model of governance which through reconciliation develops into a "community of peoples" in freedom, equality, solidarity and peace and which is deeply rooted in Christian basic values.'[3] Even Jacques Delors, the former president of the EC, spoke in July 2011 of the 'Europe of values', in whose Constitution 'Catholicism, or rather Christianity more generally, played a major role'.[4]

However, by the time Delors made his statement, the political interests associated with EU integration had become reluctant to explicitly associate their values with Christianity or, for that matter, with many of the historical traditions associated with the legacy of Europe. In response to this anti-traditional European federalist political culture, Delors observed that 'today we have hidden our shared values'. As an example he pointed to the Lisbon Treaty drawn up in 2007, in which 'several heads of governments refused to have these roots alluded to'. He added that 'this is very sad, because we need to know where we have come from'.

Confusion – or indeed, a fundamental disagreement – about the legacy of Europe and the values that define it transcends the 2012 debate between Orbán and the MEPs hostile to the policies adopted by his government. It was evident that whatever the EU meant, it was not a community of shared values. The debate also revealed that the conflict of values was far more polarizing than differences over economic or social policies. As we shall outline in the chapters to follow, the not-so-silent Culture War sweeping Europe has become the focus for some of the most important disputes in the current era.

The manner in which the 2012 debate was represented in the West European media illustrated the heightened sense of tension that surrounds conflicts over values. An article titled 'Hungary in the Crossfire; Orbán Lashes Out at Critics in European Parliament', carried by the German *Spiegel Online*, condemned Orbán's speech as a 'nationalist tirade',[5] stating that Orbán 'came across as pugnacious, dogmatic and unforgiving'. The British *Guardian* predicted that because of his speech 'Hungary PM Viktor Orbán faces EU backlash over new policies'.[6] Other media outlets cast Orbán into the role of an authoritarian demagogue and characterized Hungary as the EU's pariah state. As one columnist for the Canadian *Globe and*

Mail, writing a 'Letter on Freedom to Hungary's Viktor Orbán', asserted, 'you run a country that has become a pariah of the European Union'.[7]

One of the few Western media outlets that attempted to stand back and offer a more dispassionate account of the debate was the British *Financial Times*. In a live blog on the debate, its blogger noted that 'although there were some fireworks, they mostly came from MEPs on the ideological left and not from Orbán himself, who sat through the entire session and remained decorous throughout.' The reporter added that 'after enduring more than three hours of criticism and complaint, Orbán kept his cool in his closing'.[8]

The rhetoric of alarm conveyed by the media is itself sociologically significant. The claims that Orbán launched into a 'nationalist tirade' during the course of the debate are difficult to reconcile with the minutes of the proceedings. However, the rhetoric of condemnation was in all likelihood genuinely felt. Why? Because from the standpoint of the EU's cosmopolitan political culture, the mere hint of a positive orientation towards religious or national traditions was likely to be perceived as out of step with the culture of the new Europe. The passions and hostility that Orbán's statement incited amongst his detractors in the European Parliament and sections of the media were motivated by a genuine conviction that the Hungarian government represented a threat to what, for a lack of better expression, can be characterized as the EU way of life.

Conflicts over culture are noisy and intemperate, and many Western advocates of the EU's anti-national and federalist approach regard Orbán and his government as a unique threat to their project. As the Hungarian MEP György Schöpflin pointed out, 'There seems to be a well-established view in some parts of the European Commission that Hungary under its Fidesz government has become a tiresome member state, that it is constantly breaking the formal and the informal rules of EU membership'. Schöpflin remarked that 'this attitude seems so deeply engrained that in the eyes of some, it no longer needs any proof, but has become a starting assumption'.[9]

The Romanian Social Democratic MEP Ioan Enciu was one of the few of Orbán's critics to point explicitly to the cause of their dislike of the Hungarian government. He stated that 'from the very moment it came to power, the Hungarian government has been persisting in promoting policies that conflict with European law and have a strong nationalist-populist aspect'. From the standpoint of the political class that dominates the EU, the terms 'nationalist' and 'populist' represent maladies that afflict public life. For them, the mere mention of these terms alludes to a political culture that is antithetical to values and practices considered legitimate in Brussels.

The Culture Wars in perspective

The way that the EU political class uses the terms 'nationalist' and 'populist' has little to do with the original meaning of the terms. According to its anti-populist cultural script, nationalism is the natural companion of xenophobia. It is frequently suggested that it serves as the point of departure for the kind of aggressive nationalism that characterized the violent racist movements of the interwar era. Although the EU political class justifies its anti-nationalist rhetoric by pointing to the dangers of racist xenophobic movements and constantly harks back to the rise of the Nazis during the Weimar Republic, it is actually hostile to any form of national or patriotic sentiment. It regards people's identification with their nation as a regrettable act of prejudice. Its federalist inclination directs it to adopt a posture of animosity towards the ideal of national sovereignty.

The leadership of the EU regards the principle of national sovereignty as the driver of Euroscepticism and, therefore, as a threat to the integrity of its institutions. Speaking in this vein, Herman van Rompuy, the then president of the EU Council, told a Berlin audience in November 2010 that 'Euroscepticism leads to war', and concluded his speech with the rallying cry, 'we have to fight the danger of the new Euroscepticism'.[10] The claim that Euroscepticism represented an incitement to war was linked to the assertion that such an outlook inevitably encouraged the revival of the aggressive nationalism of the interwar era. In this speech, van Rompuy reasserted the argument that advocacy of nationalism is dangerous and national sovereignty is a 'lie'.

Hostility towards populism is underpinned by the concern that it appeals directly to the public and that its aim to mobilize the masses undermines the EU and its elitist institutions. These institutions are based on insulating decision-makers from direct public pressure so as to allow them to act in accordance with the advice from their experts. As Bulgarian political scientist Ivan Krastev observed, at the 'heart of the conflict' is 'the clash between liberal rationalism embodied by EU institutions and the populist revolt against the unaccountability of the elites'.[11] In the context of European political life, hostility towards the unaccountability of the elites frequently assumes the form of Euroscepticism – consequently, governments, and movements that express views and policies which may be construed as nationalist, populist, or Eurosceptic are likely to be condemned by the EU political class.

In this polarized landscape, any criticism of substance directed at the EU is automatically dismissed as a threat to the stability of the institutional order. In an interesting aside, the social anthropologist Maryon Macdonald, who conducted interviews with EU civil servants in Brussels, observed that there were real limits to the kind of criticisms that could be raised with them. A serious critic of the EU courted condemnation for being, by definition, a right-wing extremist. Macdonald wrote that, 'since the 1970s especially, it has become increasingly difficult in Europe to criticize the EU without appearing to be some lunatic right-wing fascist, racist or nationalist, the one often eliding with the other, or simply the parochial idiot of Little Britain.'[12] The power of this rhetoric of condemnation has, until relatively recently, been quite successful in silencing many potential critics.

East European nations anxious to join the EU understood that acceptance of this institution's anti-nationalist and anti-populist values was a non-negotiable part of the deal. As one account of the Europeanization of these former members of the Soviet bloc argues, East European political parties were instructed to model their behaviour on the *modus vivendi* of the Western cousins. If they had to form coalition governments, they were 'expected to forge enduring partnerships and avoid alliances with extremists, Euro-sceptics, and ex-authoritarians'.[13] This form of political conditionality placed parties under pressure to act in accordance with the EU consensus. According to one study, in Hungary, 'EU pressure over-rode the pivotal cleavage pitting "traditionalists" against "westernisers" and apparently 'stifled' an incipient conflict of cultural values.[14]

Domestic debates on the values that would define Hungarian society in the future were to some extent suspended in order to ensure that there were no political obstacles to becoming a member state of the EU. It was widely recognized that the precondition for former member states of the Soviet bloc to gain entry into the EU was the acceptance of a cultural script produced in Brussels.

Back in the early 1990s, during the period of negotiations regarding the terms of membership, Hungary was assigned the role of a student facing an examination on its capacity to understand and practise European values. The 'Copenhagen Criteria' outlined procedures that candidate countries to the EU had to meet before they could become members. These 'approval procedures' meant that candidate countries had to abide by the terms outlined by the European Council in Copenhagen in 1993. One criterion was the willingness of the candidate state to accept and promote European values.

The document outlining the Copenhagen criteria stated that 'any European country may apply for membership if it respects the democratic values of the EU and is committed to promoting them'.[15] Unfortunately, this vague and abstract reference to 'democratic values' lacked clarity and practical meaning. Since the rhetoric of democratic values is used by a wide variety of actors, from the Democratic People's Republic of Korea to the United States, its meaning is open to different interpretations. In practice the implication conveyed to would-be members of the EU was that they would have to endorse uncritically and abide by the political culture promoted and practised by the different institutions of the EU.

During the 1990s, all the East European candidate states went out of their way to demonstrate that they fully accepted the Copenhagen criteria and, by implication, the political authority of the EU. In the case of Hungary, virtually the entire political class signalled its willingness to be 'Europeanized'. The April 1994 memorandum accompanying Hungary's application for EU membership stated that joining this institution was a 'historical necessity' for 'which there is no real alternative'.[16] The EC welcomed this response and drew attention to a statement made by Hungary's President Árpád Göncz that endorsed 'Hungarian commitment to an ever closer political Union'.[17]

A document outlining Hungary's readiness to meet all the conditions for membership of the EU prepared by this nation's government in 1998 claimed that its political institutions had become fully Europeanized. It boasted that Hungary's 'parliamentary parties mirrored the legacy of European political culture'. The document also implied that Hungary's political system worked in accordance with the political values of the EU and pointedly noted that in neither the elections of 1990 nor those of 1994 did an extreme right-wing or left-wing party gain representation in Parliament.[18]

The social consensus adopted by the political leaders of Hungary in the late 1990s was based on the conviction that there was no alternative to an unquestioned acceptance of EU value-conditionality. At the time and subsequently, this consensus around the acceptance of EU conditionality was characterized as a triumph for liberal values. However, the procedure violated one very important principle of liberalism, which was the right to choose between alternatives. Neither the 'take it or leave it' terms offered by the EU nor the policies of the newly emergent East European political elites offered much of a choice to their citizens. Instead the population was informed that the policies and values adopted to meet the Copenhagen criteria were not so much good but necessary. Krastev observed that there was little opportunity for the people of East Europe to express reservation or disagreement with the integration process. He wrote that:

> The transition period was marked by excessive elite control over political processes and by a fear of mass politics. The accession of the Central and Eastern European countries to the EU virtually institutionalized elite hegemony over the democratic process.[19]

At the time, many East European Governments and politicians looked to their close association with the West in general and the EU in particular to legitimate their authority. For a relatively brief period of time, the politics of Europeanization kept domestic cleavages and dissidence in check. But by the turn of the twenty-first century, disappointment with the promise of regime change and Europeanization provided a fertile terrain for the flourishing of political opposition. Although criticism and opposition to the hegemony of the Westernizing transnational elite took different forms, it assumed a particularly polarizing dimension in the domain of culture. From the turn of the twenty-first century onwards, advocates of Western transnational values of the EU had to compete with those promoted by advocates of Hungarian nationalism and traditionalism.

Weak normative power of the EU

Since the 2012 exchange in the European Parliament discussed earlier, the debate on cultural values between the advocates of a federalist EU and the Orbán government have become even more polarized. As far as Orbán's old opponent Guy Verhofstadt is concerned, Hungary, and for that matter Poland, are beyond the pale. 'The sad reality is that, were they to apply for EU membership today, neither Hungary nor Poland would be admitted,' he warned in April 2016.[20] His sentiment is widely shared by pro-EU ideologues and intellectuals who regard the values advocated by the Hungarian government as a fundamental challenge to those of the EU.

Some critics of the Hungarian government go so far as to claim that it represents an existential threat to the EU. For example, Peter Wilkin of Brunel University has asserted that the policies of the Orbán regime call into question the legitimacy of the EU and therefore represents a threat to its integrity.[21] The German political scientist Jan-Werner Müller, who regularly exhorts the EU to punish Hungary for its supposed transgressions, warned that 'inaction over Hungary and Poland has undermined the elite's ability to preach "shared European values"'.[22] Critics of Hungary and, more recently, of Poland, often use an ethnocentric language that condemns not merely these nations' governments but also their people. For example Jakob Augstein, the editor of the German weekly *Freitag*, has argued for the exclusion of Poland from the EU on the grounds that this nation, like those of others in East Europe, are on the wrong side of the Culture War. Augstein argued that 'the western values of liberalism, tolerance, equality confront the eastern lack of values – racism, ignorance, bigotry'.[23]

Müller, unlike many critics of populism, has recognized that what is at stake is a conflict over values; he is particularly concerned with what he perceives as the 'diminishing' of the EU's 'normative' power.[24] However, what Müller overlooks is that the EU's normative power has always been conspicuously feeble, and that the actions of the Hungarian and Polish governments merely draw attention to a long-standing problem. In a sense, the very public assertion of the principle of national sovereignty by these governments has created an 'Emperor Has No Clothes' situation.

Since the end of the Second World War, supporters of European federalism have always been concerned about the weak normative foundation on which their project rested. From the 1950s onwards, the advocates of European integration and unification have tended to be more comfortable with promoting an economic justification for their cause than in attempting to win support for an explicit system of shared values. Throughout its history, the project of European unification gained respect and support for the economic and, to a lesser extent, geopolitical advantages that it offered. Institutions such as the old European Economic Community (EEC) took some of the credit for the continent's economic recovery in the post-Second World War era. The close cooperation of West European nations, particularly France and West Germany, were also seen as helpful for maintaining the (sometimes precarious) balance of power during the Cold War.

The problem of providing a normative foundation for the European project was evident to many leading advocates of the European federalist project. Their response in the 1950s and 1960s was to avoid an explicit engagement with the domain of values. Instead, they opted to side-step this issue. The main arguments for European unification stressed its contribution to the promotion of economic prosperity and the provision of security in the face of the Cold War. Until the 1970s, the viability of this approach was underwritten by the post-war boom, an unprecedented era of economic prosperity. The EEC, established in 1958, took the credit for the improved material conditions of Western European societies, and throughout the 1960s, its moral authority was rarely tested.

European transnational institutions were also the progeny of the Cold War. The heightened geopolitical tension during the 1950s and 1960s helped to strengthen the EEC's claim that it was essential for the maintenance of security. The launching of the EU in 1993 continued with the tradition of depoliticizing values-related issues and adopting a form of technocratic governance that relied on the claim that it played a vital role in the maintenance of economic prosperity.

In the context of the Cold War and relative economic security, the project of European unification faced relatively little pressure to justify itself in normative terms. Consequently, the capacity of its normative power to influence developments were rarely tested. Until the mid-1970s, the EEC's leaders adhered to the conviction that the benefits of economic cooperation would eventually encourage the people of Europe to identify politically with the federalist project.

However in the 1970s, advocates of the European project realized that reliance on economics alone was not enough – the formulation of a normative foundation on which the authority of their institution rested had to be addressed. Their calls for a 'new narrative for Europe' were motivated by the realization that the EU could no longer count on the Cold War to legitimize its standing indefinitely. Nor could it forever rely on the stabilizing influence of economic prosperity to retain the passive support of the public for its institutions.

Linking the fortunes of the project of European unity with the economic stability and wellbeing of member states became increasingly problematic from 1973 onwards. The economic crisis of 1973 indicated to the leadership of the EEC that it was necessary to find some kind of explicitly political or cultural justification for its existence. The leadership of the EEC responded by attempting to mobilize the resources of culture in an effort to win hearts and minds.[25]

Since the 1970s, a series of recurrent economic crises has forced the EU to try to supplement its economic authority with a series of cultural initiatives. The EU-sponsored report *The Spiritual and Cultural Dimension of Europe* of October 2004 recognized that with the end of the Cold War, economics must still continue to play an important role in legitimating the authority of the EU. Its 'Concluding Remarks', penned by Kurt Biedenkopf, Bronislaw Geremek, and Krzysztof Michalski, stated:

> As memories of the Second World War faded and the risk of conflict between the Atlantic Alliance and the Soviet Union receded, the transformation of the EEC into the European Community, and finally into the European Union, pushed the Union's economic goals ever more to the fore. Economic growth, improvement in living standards, extending and enhancing systems of social protection, and rounding off the common market assumed a priority.[26]

However, although this report emphasized the importance of economic growth for underwriting the authority of the EU, it also recognized that something else was needed to endow this institution with legitimacy.

The report concluded that the principal challenge facing the EU was a political one, and that the viability of the project of unification therefore depended on its ability to establish a political foundation for its authority. It warned that the 'internal cohesion that is necessary for the European Union' cannot be provided by 'economic forces alone':

It is no coincidence that economic integration is not enough to drive European political reform. Economic integration simply does not, of itself, lead to political integration because markets cannot produce a politically resilient solidarity. Solidarity – a genuine sense of civic community – is vital because the competition that dominates the marketplace gives rise to powerful centrifugal forces. Markets may create the economic basis of a polity and are thereby an indispensable condition of its political constitution. But they cannot on their own produce political integration and provide a constitutive infrastructure for the Union. The original expectation, that the political unity of the EU would be a consequence of the European common market has proven to be illusory.[27]

In pointing out the limits of economics for maintaining and developing the political unity of the EU, the authors of this report echoed the pithy statement made previously by Jacques Delors, former president of the EC, who noted in his essay, 'Our Europe', that 'nobody falls in love with a growth rate'.

A report published by the EU in 2013 titled *New Narrative for Europe*, and the publication *Mind and Body of Europe: New Narrative*, explicitly recognized that the end of the Cold War represented a challenge to the standing and relevance of the EU. The Luxembourg MEP and prominent advocate of the EU, Viviane Reding, stated that:

> In recent years, the experiences of war, of totalitarian regimes and the Cold War have gradually lost their immediacy in the eyes of the general public, which is to say that those horrors are losing their legitimising force. More and more Europeans regard the experiences of the 20th century – rightly or wrongly – as a thing of the past. The alarming results of the most recent European elections are proof of this trend: the fact that 25 % of the European electorate voted for extremist and anti-European parties shows that they must have somehow 'forgotten' the reasons for which the European Union was built. This presents a particular challenge for a new narrative for future European integration. It needs to give 'heart and soul' to Europe and help prevent people from repeating the mistakes of the past as citizens are increasingly swayed by dangerous, populist rabble-rouser.[28]

The call for a new narrative for European unity was motivated by the understanding that the EU could no longer rely on the passive acquiescence of the European public, and that the practice of technocratic governance needed to be supplemented by a political narrative that could capture the imagination of citizens. But since values that could legitimate the EU cannot simply be plucked out of thin air, finding the 'heart and soul' of Europe proved to be a constantly elusive quest.

At the time Barroso, the president of the EC, argued that the era of passive acquiescence or what he called 'implicit consent' had to be replaced by a more explicit engagement with public life. He informed his audience at the State of the Union conference in May 2013:

> We are at a point in time when European integration must be pursued openly, transparently and with the explicit support of the citizens of Europe. The times of European integration by implicit consent of citizens are over. Europe has to be ever more democratic. Europe's democratic legitimacy and accountability must keep pace with its increased role and power.[29]

For Barroso, the concept of implicit consent implied a state of affairs where European institutions were spared the task of having to gain the endorsement of the public as its legitimate authority. Barroso's statement on the end of implicit consent raised the question of how to inspire people to adopt a more explicit identification with the EU. Unfortunately the answer that the EU leadership offered to this question was not, as Barroso suggested, more democracy – rather, it was the use of the public relations practice of rebranding the EU through a 'new narrative'.

Rendering values explicit

Barroso's statement regarding the EU's legitimacy deficit indicated that the question of European values was far more problematic than he implied in his January 2012 exchange with Viktor Orbán. Barroso was in no doubt that 'the politics of implicit consent' were over and that the 'peace, prosperity and democracy' that had legitimized the EU in the past could no longer motivate the younger generations.[30] While Barroso recognized that the problem of the EU's legitimacy deficit had to be confronted, he could provide no solution for it, since this would have required an explicit engagement with the question of the normative foundation on which this institution rested.

The problem with the Hungarian government was not so much its advocacy of traditional values but that it raised questions to do with the domain of the normative in the first place. Avoiding the domain of the normative was integral to the practice of implicit consent, and Hungary's approach to values threatened to open up a can of worms.

The reluctance to address the thorny question of Europe's foundational values has been a long-standing practice in the EU. As noted previously, Jacques Delors drew attention to the EU's reluctance to engage with this problem openly, when he stated back in 2010 that 'today we have hidden our shared values'. In this remarkable statement, Delors explicitly criticized the leadership of the EU, argued that the EU leadership's failure to uphold Europe's values would have drastic consequences in the future. He asserted;

> I do not know where the frontiers of this Europe of values are to be found but, from an intellectual viewpoint, European society does exist, even though today we have hidden our shared values. We have done so on the one hand

because we are terrified by globalisation and, on the other, because we are developing a kind of individualism that is made worse by a world character-ized by media coverage and a kind of politics based on public opinion polls. All those values that go to make up a society are being done away with; day after day they are being destroyed. If the values of Europe are in decline, then it is Europe that suffers.[31]

Delors' concern about political leaders' apparent indifference to Europe's shared historical values was particularly directed at the casual manner with which they ignored the cultural legacy of the continent's past. His statement directly touched on the issues that were later raised in the debate on Hungary in the European Parliament in January 2012. As if responding to the statement by French MEP Marie-Christine Vergiat that 'European values are not Christian values', Delors remarked that on the contrary, 'Catholicism, or rather Christianity more generally, played a major role in the Europe of values'.

The one question that neither Barroso nor Delors addressed is, why? Why were Europe's shared values hidden by political leaders committed to the cause of European unification? Arguably this was the issue that fuelled the highly charged and polarized debate that erupted in the 2012 debate. As we explain later, from 1945 onwards, the project of European unification was entwined with the aspiration to break away from the legacy of the past – including the traditions and values that were associated with the history of this continent. Initially this aspiration was motivated by a reaction to Europe's troubled and often violent past. The pioneers of European unification were determined to distance their project from the influences that led to the outbreak of two world wars. With the passing of time, their attempt to distance Europe from its legacy of conflict hardened into an attitude that regarded the values and traditions of the past with suspicion. Consequently, instead of forging an authority based on the values of Europe's tradition, the founders of the EU looked to expert and technocratic authority for gaining legitimacy.

Traditional values were not so much explicitly rejected as evaded and depo-liticized. In the post-Second World War era, the status of tradition and many of the values associated with it acquired negative connotations in Western public discourse. The standing of traditional values further diminished in the 1960s. One of the accomplishments of the 1960s cultural revolution was to provide an explicit narrative for the devaluation of traditional norms and practices. In many quarters traditional norms and values were portrayed as expressions of outdated prejudice. Referring to this development, the historian Eric Hobsbawm wrote of a 'cultural revolution', which he described as 'the breaking of the threads which in the past had woven human beings into social textures'. Hobsbawm stated that as a result, 'what children could learn from parents became less obvious than what parents did not know and children did'.[32]

Supporters of tradition were clearly on the defensive and, according to the chair of the Adenauer Foundation, 'the revolt of 1968 destroyed more values than did the

Third Reich'.[33] It was clear to many conservative thinkers that by this time, these values could only survive on life-support. For the British historian J. H. Plumb, the widespread derision of 'hollow' values confirmed *The Death of the Past*. In a lecture given in 1968, he told his audience that 'wherever we look, in all areas of social and personal life, the hold of the past is weakening'.[34] Indeed for many, the past had ceased to be a repository of meaningful values with which to influence and socialize the younger generations.

One of the consequences of exiling the past and its traditions from public life was the growing tendency to adopt a public language that eschewed statements of values and moral norms. In Western European public life, arguments and statements that are communicated through a self-consciously moral language are rarely taken seriously in their own terms. This trend is particularly evident in communications within academic circles and cultural elites. In academic literature, morally framed arguments tend to be treated with contempt and scorn. The sociologists Shai Dromi and Eva Illouz point to a tendency to de-legitimate morality as a subject that ought to be taken seriously and to a 'widespread conflation of morality with coercive ideological structures'.[35] The historian David Rowe echoes this point, contending that in some cases, the term 'moral' is deployed to signify that a particular phenomenon should not be taken seriously. He wrote that the coupling of the adjective 'moral' with the noun 'panic' offers 'a pejorative connotative dimension'.[36]

Because in the current cultural climate issues that touch on the domain of the moral are perceived by policy makers as divisive and disruptive, they tend to be avoided. Often their reluctance to engage explicitly with moral issues is expressed through a technical language that insists that what matters is what the evidence shows rather than the a priori claim of what is right and wrong. Often this approach is justified by the claim that morality is at best an outdated form of false consciousness and at worst a coercive ideological construct. So it is not surprising that sections of the EU's political elite have elected to hide Europe's shared values. The moral language of right and wrong and good and evil are often rejected on the grounds that they are too judgmental. Politics often used a non-judgmental and morally neutral technical vocabulary so that decisions are justified as being 'evidence based' and founded upon 'research'.

Debates about values often acquire an acrimonious character. As the American political theorist Francis Fukuyama noted, 'conflicts over "values" are potentially much more deadly than conflicts over material possessions or wealth'.[37] But the hostility directed towards Orbán and the Constitution enacted by his government was not simply directed at the values it endorsed but the very fact that by its actions, Hungary had placed the question of values back on the political agenda. And many EU politicians fear that a serious debate on moral norms runs the risk of isolating them from a significant section of the people of Europe.

In a conversation conducted with the *Frankfurter Allgemeine Zeitung* a couple of months after the 2012 European Parliament debate, Orbán was reminded by his interviewer: 'Mr Prime Minister, you are being criticised by the EU institutions in Brussels like no head of government.' Orbán's explanation about the hostility directed at him was focused on his opponents' determination to ensure that Europe's shared values remain hidden. 'There is something that I call a hidden or a secret Europe', he remarked. 'I have this feeling that for the sake of the debate over cultural and political correctness we no longer speak about the topics that are necessary so that we can continue to exist as a crucial civilisation.'[38]

In a sense, the questions raised by the journalist from the *Frankfurter Allgemeine Zeitung* pointed to two distinct but interrelated issues. One was that of the status of traditional values, such as nation, family, and the role of religion; the other was the willingness to discuss these issues openly and to render explicit Europe's relation with its past. For better or worse, the Hungarian Constitution, and especially its historical preamble, is self-consciously directed at affirming the authority of the past. In contrast, the EU has found it difficult to reconcile its vision of the future with its history. Despite considerable efforts, the EU's attempt to elaborate on 'A New Narrative for Europe' fails to point out what was the 'old narrative'. Nor is it able to project a Europe that is organically related to what went before.[39] Indeed, judging by many of the statements made by its political and intellectual advocates, the launching of the project of European unification is often depicted as an act of negating Europe's past.

The problem of the past

The contrast between the new Hungarian Constitution and the one that it replaced mirrors the difference between attitudes towards the values of the past expressed during the 2012 debate in the European Parliament. The 1989 Hungarian Constitution that emerged in the aftermath of this nation's transition from the Stalinist era was the product of deliberations that sought to avoid the dealing with the question of the relationship between Hungary's past and present predicament. This 1989 Constitution was founded not on the historical traditions of Hungarian society, but on what one of its most ardent Western supporters, the Princeton University sociologist Kim Lane Scheppele, has characterized as 'transnational constitutionalism'.[40]

Transnational constitutionalism 'takes its inspiration from internationally respected norms of human rights' and from rules and procedures advocated by international organizations. The appeal of transnational ideals for its Hungarian supporters was that they bypassed the question, what is the foundation for the authority of Hungary's Constitution? As far as the authors of the 1989 Constitution were concerned, one of its virtues was that it provided a breathing space, during which the more profound question of the relationship between Hungary's past and the present could be evaded.

Transnational constitutionalism emerged in the post-Second World War era and paralleled the 'shift of emphasis from substantive to procedural sources of authority' in Western societies.[41] Transnational constitutionalism presents itself as a value-neutral expression of the rule of law. András Bozóki, a former minister of culture, has praised the '1989 democratic constitution' because of its value-neutrality. He contends that the 1989 Constitution was 'ideologically neutral'. He criticizes the new Constitution on the grounds that it 'features one of the longest preambles in Europe, composed of a whopping 26 paragraphs', which serves as an expression of a 'national religious belief system'.[42] It is anything but a neutral document.

Supporters of the new Constitution, the Fundamental Law, argue that the connection that the preamble of this document draws between the present and its long-standing historical traditions is underpinned by a legitimate concern to uphold and celebrate the nation's cultural and moral legacy. The Hungarian conservative philosopher, Ferenc Hörcher, contends that 'it is through the preamble that the text of the constitution tries to connect the neutral state institutions with society's cultural-moral order, in this way making it possible for trust to accumulate towards it'.[43]

Hörcher's argument raises important questions about the relation of values to the authority of the law. He criticizes the 1989 Constitution on the ground that because of the reluctance of its authors to engage with the realm of values it failed to confront the question of how to forge a relationship of trust between citizens and government. Hörcher appears to suggest that during the period of regime change, when Hungary had to abide by the rules set by Western international organizations, there was little choice but to opt for a so-called value-neutral constitutional arrangement. However, he believes that short-term expediency on the values questions had a corrosive impact on the legitimacy of the new system, arguing that, 'in the long run the system's value deficit played a major role in delegitimizing the political system'.[44]

It is important to point out that despite the claim of value-neutrality, constitutional arrangements are rarely neutral. They may be silent on the question of values and hold them implicitly, but in debates about constitutional arrangements there are always values at stake. The very fact that in its debate of Hungary, the European Parliament raised the question of whether or not the Constitution violated the EU's values was an implicit recognition of the fact that it was far from value-neutral.

The current debate on European values and of their relation to the policies of the Hungarian government and its Constitution do not simply reflect a clash of cultural attitudes towards everyday issues in political and public life. They raise fundamental questions that touch on the legitimacy of political institutions and, ultimately, on the foundation on which the social and moral order is constituted. Since the acquisition of legitimacy remains one of the most important challenges facing all European governments, the problems raised in the European Parliamentary debate on Hungary has continued to serve as a focus of conflict.

During the years following this debate, the actions of the Hungarian government continued to be seen as a threat to the viability of democracy not only within the nation but also within the EU.[45] However, even though many European federalists may not like what they see in Hungary, they know that the conflict over values will not go away. Sooner or later they too will have to engage with the question of what are the values that binds their society together.

Notes

1   For a record of these debates see www.europarl.europa.eu/sides/getDoc.do?pubRef=-//
    EP//TEXT+CRE+20120118+ITEM-021+DOC+XML+V0//EN.
2   See www.europarl.europa.eu/sides/getDoc.do?pubRef=-//EP//TEXT+CRE+20120118+
    ITEM-021+DOC+XML+V0//EN.
3   Fountain, J. (2011) 'A Christian Europe(an): The Forgotten Vision of Robert Shuman',
    The Schuman Centre for European Studies, Netherlands, Encounters Mission Journal, no. 36,
    March 2011, https://encountersmissionjournal.files.wordpress.com/2011/08/fountain_
    2011-03_schumann_and_europe.pdf.
4   See his statement on www.eurozine.com/articles/2011-07-01-delors-en.html.
5   Verseck, K, (2012) 'Hungary in the Crossfire: Orbán Lashes Out at Critics in European
    Parliament', 19 January 2012, www.spiegel.de/international/europe/hungary-in-the-
    crossfire-orban-lashes-out-at-critics-in-european-parliament-a-810062.html.
6   www.theguardian.com/world/2012/jan/18/hungary-viktor-orban-eu-backlash.
7   Peter, K. (2012) 'A Letter on freedom to Hungary's Viktor Orbán', *The Globe and Mail*,
    26 January 2012.
8   Peter, S (2012) 'Live Blog: Viktor Orbán at the EU parliament', 18 January 2012,
    http://blogs.ft.com/brusselsblog/2012/01/18/live-blog-viktor-orban-at-the-eu-
    parliament/
9   Schöpflin, G. 'Hungary and the EU: A Troubled Relationship', *Politico*, 11 July 2012,
    www.politico.eu/article/hungary-and-the-eu-a-troubled-relationship/
10 Waterfield, B. (2010) 'Herman Van Rompuy: 'Euroscepticism Leads to War', *The Daily
    Telegraph*, 10 November 2010.
11 Krastev (2007).
12 McDonald (2005) p. 4.
13 Mikulova (2013) p. 167.
14 Mikulova (2013) p. 167.
15 See 'Coppenhagen criteria', http://ec.europa.eu/enlargement/policy/conditions-
    membership/index_en.htm.
16 Cited in 'Commission Opinion on Hungary's Application for Membership of the Euro-
    pean Union', *DOC/97/13 Brussels*, 15 July 1997, file:///Users/frankfuredi/Downloads/
    DOC-97–13_EN%20(1).pdf
17 *ibid.*
18 Magyar Köztársoság Kulugyminiszterium as a Integrácios Stratégiai Munkacsoport (1998)
    *Magyarország a '90-es években: A Magyar kormany válasza az Europai Unió kérdöivére – rövidett
    változat*, Budapest, p. 9.
19 Krastev (2007)
20 www.project-syndicate.org/columnist/guy-verhofstadt.
21 Wilkin is cited in, 'EU faces 'crisis of legitimacy' as Hungary's far-right continues to push
    against migrants', *The Daily Express*, 12 November, 2016.
22 www.lrb.co.uk/v38/n11/jan-werner-muller/europes-sullen-child.
23 Cited by Weiss, C. (2016) 'German Politicians and Media Agitate against Poland', 12 January
    2016, www.wsws.org/en/articles/2016/01/12/pola-j12.html.
24 www.lrb.co.uk/v38/n11/jan-werner-muller/europes-sullen-child.
25 See Kaiser (2015) p. 374.
26 https://ec.europa.eu/research/social-sciences/pdf/other_pubs/michalski_091104_report_
    annexes_en.pdf.
27 https://ec.europa.eu/research/social-sciences/pdf/other_pubs/michalski_091104_report_
    annexes_en.pdf.
28 Viviane Reding Stimulating the European Public Space (2013) in *Mind and Body of Europe:
    New Narrative*.
29 Speech by President Barroso at the State of the Union conference: Restoring confidence
    9 May 2013, http://europa.eu/rapid/press-release_SPEECH-13-397_en.htm.
30 Barossso is cited in Kaiser (2015) p. 367.

31 See 'An interview with Jacques Delors', 8 September, 2010, by Nikola Tietze and Ulrich Bielefeld, *Mittelweg*, 36, published by *Eurozine* www.eurozine.com/articles/2011-07-01-delors-en.html.

32 Hobsbawn (2004) pp. 327 & 334.

33 Cited in *The Nation*; 22 May 1989.

34 Plumb (1989) p. 66.

35 Dromi & Illouz (2010) p. 351.

36 Rowe (2009) p. 23.

37 Fukuyama (1992) p. 214.

38 For Orbán's interview, see *Frankfurter Allgemeine Zeitung*, 4th March 2012.

39 See discussion in Kaiser (2015) pp. 367–368.

40 Scheppele (2000)

41 Spiro (1958) p. 54.

42 Bozoki, A. (2012) 'The Crisis of Democracy in Hungary', 21 May, Heinrich Böll Stiftung, www.boell.de/de/node/276334.

43 Hörcher (2014) p. 356.

44 Hörcher (2014) p. 355.

45 See the argument contained in Europe's Other Democratic Deficit: National Authoritarianism in a Democratic Union R. Daniel Kelemen Professor and Jean Monnet Chair Department of Political Science, Rutgers University, Paper presented at the Council for European Studies, 22nd International Conference of Europeanists, July 8–10, 2015 Sciences Po, Paris, France http://citeseerx.ist.psu.edu/viewdoc/download?doi=10.1.1.716.8922&rep=rep1&type=pdf

2

WHY HIDE OUR SHARED VALUES?

The problem of tradition

Jacques Delors' concern about the EU leadership's tendency to hide Europe's 'shared values' has important implications for understanding the cultural conflict and arguments that dominate Brussels' relationship with Hungary. Pro-EU techno-crats and intellectuals often regard European values and traditions that have evolved over the centuries as not only irrelevant to the needs of the twenty-first century, but also as deeply problematic and flawed. Many current advocates of European federal-ism frequently cast the cultural legacy and traditions of Europe's past, including its values, in a negative light. From this standpoint, the past is perceived as a strange and dangerous territory, whose values and practices must not be allowed to influence contemporary public life.

The anti-populist cultural script decries the traditionalist inclinations of its foes. One criticism that anti-populists hurl at their opponents is that 'populist ideol-ogy relies heavily on nostalgia'. According to the anti-populist imagination, people drawn towards populism are so uncritical of the past that they naively perceive it as a golden age of community harmony. This cultural script claims that 'misguided faith in ideas that defined people's attachment to history and tradition' leads populists to possess a distorted sense of contemporary reality.[1] The premise of the anti-populist critique of nostalgia is that rather than providing a positive guide to life, the cus-toms and traditions of the past stand for negative and oppressive conventions and practices.

This critique of nostalgia is actually imprisoned within the walls of presentism. Its devaluation of the past has as its corollary, an uncritical embrace of the present. It expresses the latter-day sentiment of Voltaire's Dr Pangloss, who naively declares that we live 'in the best of all possible worlds'. According to one commentator:

> Those who look back at the 1930s or 1960s with nostalgia invariably end up
> voting for Trump, Putin, Brexit, or the swarm of populist nationalists besieging

the European Union. People on the other side of the barricade – weak and naive as they may be – want the world to keep moving forward as it did during the post World War II era.[2]

The use of the term swarm is illustrative of the rhetoric of dehumanisation applied towards nostalgic populists. What is interesting about this commentary is that its target is not only nostalgia for the 1930s, but also the 1960s. Apparently nostalgic populists seek to hide behind old traditions and have eyes only for the past.

This deep-seated mistrust of tradition goes so far as to warn mothers and fathers to be wary of the childrearing practices used by parents in previous times. Instead, so-called parenting professionals advise mothers and fathers to heed the advice of childrearing 'experts'. In Western societies, this silent crusade against the past directs its energy towards altering the way that the adult world socializes young people. The advice and views of grandparents is frequently disregarded as irrelevant and possibly prejudicial to the healthy development of the child. As a result of the institutionalization of these attitudes, children are frequently not socialized into the values held by their ancestors.

This anti-populist and anti-traditionalist attitude towards the past is far less influential within the cultural outlook that prevails in Hungary. The ideology and the cultural practices of the Hungarian Soviet puppet regime were deeply hostile to attempts to discuss and reflect on this nation's past. Not surprisingly, people's aspiration for breaking from their 40 years of Stalinist past was in part expressed through the desire to recover the historic traditions associated with the identity of being Hungarian. For better or worse, millions of Hungarians believe that there is something distinct about their identity and way of life and many of them take the view that it is worthwhile to preserve and keep alive their heritage.

The patterns of alienation of Western European societies from their past and traditional practices are far less evident in Eastern Europe. Contrary to the interpretation advanced by the anti-populist cultural script, it is not nostalgia that inspires people's interest in the past. They know that very many bad things have occurred throughout their nation's history, but nevertheless feel that their historical legacy is in part what makes them who they are. Such sentiments provide a cultural terrain where traditional values are seen to possess meaning. Consequently, even if the Hungarian government had not enacted a new constitution, it is likely that cultural disputes between Brussels and Budapest would have erupted because of their divergent attitudes towards the authority of the past and the value of tradition.

The problem of tradition

The anti-traditionalist ethos that pervades the technocratic outlook of EU institutions is rarely spelled out explicitly in their policy statements. Indeed, the EU routinely sponsors festivals celebrating Europe's heritage or the architectural, artistic, and scientific achievements of the past. Its anti-traditionalism is directed at traditional customs and values – particularly those associated with the nation and religion. A more thoroughgoing critique of tradition is usually left to EU-phile intellectuals and, in particular, academics. In recent decades, the eminent German philosopher Jürgen Habermas has been at the forefront of providing a systematic and sophisticated exposition of the anti-populist critique of tradition.

Habermas is an erudite and politically-committed ideologue of the EU, who fully endorses this institution's criticisms of Hungary and has argued that its government is striving to create an illegitimate political order.[3] His hostility to the Hungarian government and to movements that he considers to be populist is reinforced by a political outlook that explicitly calls into question the relevance of the values of the past for contemporary times. His dislike of tradition is particularly directed at national values, which his writings constantly criticize.

Habermas has been an energetic advocate of an ideological project that aims to distance people from their national communities. One of the ways in which this project is pursued is through the advocacy of identity politics and the rights of minorities, which are promoted at the expense of the right of nations to self-determination. He is an enthusiastic proponent of social and cultural identities that stand in opposition to, or are decoupled from, national sentiments and traditions. His preference is for identities that are 'post-traditional' and 'post-national'.

At first sight, Habermas' affinity for the 'politics of recognition' and its affirmation of diverse identities seems inconsistent with his commitment to a cosmopolitan outlook. However like many members of the current generation of cosmopolitan intellectuals, his worldview has little in common with the classical Kantian ideal of a cosmopolitan world citizen. His is a negative theory of cosmopolitanism that is principally animated by a dislike for the consciousness of nationhood, rather than a positive utopian ideal of world citizenship.

Habermas' concept of post-national identity is, as one of his supporters argues, 'post-historical', one that is 'not defined by reference to the past'. It is also an identity that is clearly 'not focused on cultural traditions'.[4] On the contrary, he advocates a 'post-traditional identity' – one that has been freed from the traditions of the past and offers an alternative to it.[5] For Habermas, one of the main merits of the EU is that it is an institution that represents a reaction to Europe's past and does not draw on its traditions to validate its policies. He claims that his aversion to the traditions of the past is a justified reaction to the cycle of destructive violence unleashed by nationalist politics that culminated with the horrors of Nazi Germany. Habermas goes so far as to argue that, after the tragedy of Auschwitz, 'unquestioned traditions' and sentiments based on 'historical continuities' have become unsupportable.[6]

Habermas' use of the term 'unquestioned tradition' is important for supporting his thesis that support for tradition involves an uncritical and unthinking mindset. The word 'unquestioned' devalues the concept of tradition and is integral to his rhetorical strategy of representing it as an object of identification for the passive, uncritical, unthinking, and authoritarian mind. From this standpoint the valuation of historical symbols of nationhood, community, and religious rituals and cultural practices for their own sake is perceived as an irrational rejection of reason and of tolerant citizenship. It is worth noting that 'unquestioned beliefs' has become a central trope used by anti-traditionalist academics in their critique of those who are at all sympathetic to the traditions of the past. Professor Jan-Werner Müller, also a critic of Hungarian populism, uses the term 'unquestioned' to denounce those who allegedly embrace 'unquestioned inherited beliefs'.[7] Müller, like Habermas, seems unwilling to imagine that those who take inherited beliefs seriously can also question them.

Yet, as I have discussed in my study of the sociology of tradition, inherited beliefs have rarely been embraced uncritically. Even in the medieval era, they were questioned and tested.[8] The obsession with 'unquestioned' traditions is, in part, an outcome of a loss of historical imagination – it fails to grasp the process through which traditions change and mutate and adapt to new circumstances. Since the concept of tradition conveys so many after-the-event assumptions in the modern imagination, it can often be caricatured as a static dogma. But the medieval experience indicates that tradition is not so much a stand-alone doctrine as an orientation towards the world where the consciousness of history exists in a relatively restricted form.

Within this context, there was scope for change and innovation but in a way that was consistent with what the sociologist Edward Shils has characterized as substantive traditionality: 'the appreciation of the accomplishments and wisdom of the past and of the institutions especially impregnated with tradition, as well as the desirability of regarding patterns inherited from the past as valid guides'.[9] Unexpected threats, opportunities, and problems confronted medieval Europe no less than in modern times, and people had to engage in acts of interpretation and construct solutions to the problems of the time. This process is most usefully conceptualized as one of change within a traditionalist setting, where individuals drew on their understanding of the legacy of the past and attempted to reconcile it with their own experience. They used reason to attempt to resolve the tension between the received wisdom of eternal truths and the experience that confronted them. In the twenty-first century, where eternal truths are continually subject to contestation, even the most conservative mind understands that traditions need to adapt to changing circumstances.

The type of argument put forward by Habermas can, in one sense, be interpreted as merely a version of the rationalist anti-traditional outlook that emerged in the nineteenth century and gained ascendancy in Western societies during the course of the twentieth century. However, his version of anti-traditionalism is distinct in one very important respect. His writings convey the implication that unquestioned traditionalism is not only irrational but also has negative and destructive consequences. In particular, he implies that traditionalism logically leads to the kind of authoritarian personality that supported the Nazi regime, and that after the experience of Nazi Germany, the values embodied by tradition can no longer be trusted. As Habermas explained:

> Tradition means, after all, that we continue something as unproblematic, which others have started and demonstrated. We normally imagine that these 'predecessors', if they stood before us face to face, could not completely deceive us,

that they could not play the role of a *deus malignus*. I for one think that this basis of trust has been destroyed by the gas chambers.[10]

From this perspective, the tragedy of the Holocaust invalidates arguments and ideals that are based on an appeal to tradition.

As it happens the Holocaust, and the murderous behaviour of the Nazi Regime has little to do with tradition. As Hannah Arendt eloquently argued in her remarkable study, *The Origins of Totalitarianism*, the phenomenon of totalitarianism constituted a break from the continuity of Western history and its tradition.[11] So if anything, the tragedy of the Holocaust demands a reaffirmation of the traditions that were violated by the totalitarian moment in Europe's history. Paradoxically, the unequivocal rejection of tradition is usually associated with *Brave New World* type totalitarian regimes.

For Habermas, 'unquestioned traditions' constitute the point of departure for a teleology of evil that portrays the gas chambers as their inexorable consequence. This teleology of evil is supported by the anachronistic methodology of reading history backwards and discovering that most roads in Europe led to Auschwitz. This fatalistic theory of malevolence has been adopted in public controversies surrounding the rise of populist movements in Europe in recent years and is expressed by the slogan, 'The Holocaust did not begin with gas chambers – it began with words'. According to this logic, just about any distressing event that chronologically preceded the Holocaust bears a measure of responsibility for it.

Habermas' preference is for what he calls a 'constructivist perspective' relies on constructed norms to reign in and tame the traditional values of citizens. His language often communicates a paternalistic social engineering ambition, which is justified through the idiom of a civilizing mission: he assigns to the EU the role of a 'civilizing state power'.[12] According to the teleology of evil, just as all roads led to the Holocaust in the past, so today all manifestations of traditionalism, nationalism, and populism lead forward to the reoccurrence of this tragedy. Habermas advocates a doctrine towards the state that he describes as *constitutional patriotism*. This doctrine was elaborated to protect society from a repetition of the rise of totalitarian mass movements, and it is also mobilized to counter and negate a traditionalist outlook.

But how can the influence of traditional values be diminished? Habermas clearly understands that traditional ideals that touch on religion, nation, and family life cannot be simply abolished or transcended. Consequently, he opts for an approach that encourages a climate of scepticism towards the status and moral authority of the values of tradition. Through encouraging the questioning of people's values and identities, anti-populist theorists hope that this process weakens people's relationship to long-established traditions. Through this strategy Habermas hopes to cultivate the 'rationalization of collective identities', which is another way of saying that identities will be distanced from their foundation in tradition and continually recast on the basis of reason and rational debate. As one of Habermas' co-thinkers explains, such 'identities were most likely to emerge where national traditions had been put decisively into question and where citizens felt acutely ambivalent about affirming historical continuities'.[13]

From the perspective of critics of present-day Hungarian political culture, the attempt to uphold and promote national traditions and identity constitutes a form of disturbing cultural pathology. Kim Lane Scheppele's description of the Hungarian Parliamentary debate on whether or not the Holy Crown of Saint Stephen should serve as the symbol of the state comes across as the twenty-first-century version of a nineteenth-century colonial report on the exotic rituals of backwards savages.[14] Like Habermas, Scheppele seems to believe that after Auschwitz, the attempt to uphold traditions that symbolize a continuity with the past is inherently illegitimate. She denounces the 'dark forces of conservatism and modern fascism' for whom the 'crown represented Hungary's continuity with history'.

For Scheppele, it is the aspiration to forge continuity with the past that represents the nub of the problem. According to her reasoning, such an aspiration is likely to lead to the revival of the authoritarian and extreme nationalistic values of the bad old days. Thus she warns that the Holy Crown of Saint Stephen 'has become a symbol concentrating the dark passions of Hungarian conservatism, particularly those that move towards fascism'.[15] Her casual, almost effortless, linkage of Hungarian conservatism with fascism illustrates a disturbing tendency to weaponize the memory of the tragedy of the Second World War in a cultural crusade against the traditions of the past.

According to the single-minded, anti-national outlook offered by Habermas and Scheppele, the attempt to find meaning through the forging of symbolic continuities with the past always leads to a journey back to the Weimar Republic. In this respect, their estrangement from and hostility to the past, and their aspiration for a post-history identity, captures the *zeitgeist* that prevails in wider Western cultural life. Even a relatively successful nation such as Britain has become uncomfortable about celebrating its traditions and historical legacy. The waving of the Union Jack is frequently portrayed as an act of jingoism perpetrated by far-right extremists, and educators often denounce the teaching of national history as far too patriotic.[16] A study on Britain's political culture titled *Risk, Threat and Security* points out that this nation's people have become alienated from their national institutions and their attachment to shared values is too superficial to constitute a 'dynamic community'.[17]

In many other parts of the Western world, the display of historical and national symbols is frowned upon. It is worth noting that in the aftermath of the election of American presidential candidate Donald Trump, students at several universities burnt their nation's flag. At one institution, Hampshire College in Massachusetts, the college officials decided to placate students and faculty, who were disturbed by Trump's election by lowering the American flag.[18] In several institutions of higher education, officials described the flying of the flag as 'divisive' since some members of their university communities regard it as a symbol of 'racism and hatred'.[19] Although the burning of a national flag in Western societies is a relatively rare and unusual act of political protest, the sentiments that underpin it are not unconnected to their society's estrangement from symbols of nationhood and historical continuity.

In the interwar era, the German sociologist Ferdinand Tönnies pointed to the tendency of modernist technocratic institutions to react to the customs and traditions of community life with 'veiled hatred and contempt'.[20] This point was confirmed in 1972 by the American political scientist C. J. Friedrich, who in his fascinating review of this development observed, that 'in the twentieth century tradition became a pejorative term'.[21] Since the end of the Second World War, and especially since the 1960s, this sentiment of intolerant anti-traditionalist scorn has become increasingly directed towards those who refused to move along with the times and adopt a post-traditional identity. This attitude is explicitly committed to distancing itself morally from the past, and to rupturing the links that bind society to its historical traditions. For Habermas, this approach leads to a 'sobered political identity', one that has 'detached itself from the background of a past centred on national history'. He also welcomes this identity because it has ceased to be 'sworn to triumphal continuities'.[22]

There is one crucial difference between the anti-traditionalist temper of the twenty-first century and that of the past. Historically, anti-traditionalism sought to bring about a positive change in the working of society. The current hostility towards tradition is directed at celebrating the present and upholding the values that prevail today. In this sense, despite its anti-conservative rhetoric, current anti-traditionalism possesses no ambition to bring about a different world in the future.

Although the post-traditional and post-national sentiments outlined by Habermas have not yet captured the popular imagination of Western societies, they exercise considerable influence over their cultural elites and institutions. That is why, from their standpoint, the refusal of Hungary and other East European societies to reject an identity rooted in national sentiment and a 'past centred on national history' is perceived as a political malady that needs to be cured by enlightened social engineers. For Habermas such an intervention requires the services of a civilizing institution such as the EU. From this perspective a populist can never be a responsible citizen; they should always be considered an immature child in need of paternalistic enlightenment.

Since the turn of the twenty-first century, the EU has devoted considerable resources towards attempting to realign the political culture of East European societies like Hungary in line with its anti-traditionalist ethos. Numerous studies have drawn attention to what can best be described as a neo-colonialist impulse to impose EU values on the new East European member states. According to Ian Klinke, such studies have 'highlighted the neo-colonial overtones that reverberate throughout the EU's Eastern enlargement, particularly through the ideologically coloured aims of "Europeanising", "modernising" and "liberalising" a space that was deemed economically and politically inferior'.[23]

The EU's Jean Monnet Programme, designed to promote European integration through influencing academic institutions and exchanges, has often blurred the line between disinterested research and political advocacy. Oriane Calliagro's study *Negotiating Europe: The EU Promotion of Europeanness since 1950* shows that this programme explicitly encouraged a de-territorialized version of European history.[24] A review of the activities of the Jean Monnet Programme suggest that one of its objectives was to counter and neutralize the influence of tradition in the intellectual and cultural life of East Europe. Klinke cites Erhard Bussek, Monnet chair and special coordinator of the Stability Pact for South Eastern Europe, stating in 2009 that the programme would help alleviate the 'weakness of the traditional systems' of East Europe. Klinke concludes that 'this framing of accession states as traditional and weak reinforces arguments about the EU's neo-colonial gaze upon the East'.[25]

Some radical critics of the EU's attempt to impose its values on new member states have used the term 'normative imperialism' to highlight what can most accurately be described as a project of cultural domination.[26] However, the EU's tendency to impose its norms on member states, particularly those of East Europe, should not be seen as an example of a confident act of projecting cultural power. The EU oligarchy is strikingly defensive about its normative power. It is aware that it continually faces a legitimacy deficit and has failed to win the loyalty of European citizens.

As we discuss later in this book, the attempt to counter traditional and nationalist influences is not solely directed at Eastern Europe but also at the wider European public. Indeed as the EU's current propaganda campaign against populism indicates, its normative hegemony is also questioned within the societies of Western Europe.

The power of the Crown

Many sociological studies of Hungarian national identity concur that, despite the expectation that this would weaken in the post-communist era, it continues to flourish. As one study of this phenomenon, published in 2008, acknowledged, 'today's public opinion in Hungary is infused with intense spontaneous national identity'.[27] The study also noted that 'cultural-historical rhetoric still determines national discourse'. The word 'still' is interesting, for it conveys the idea that a 'cultural-historical rhetoric' contradicts the ethos of a modernizing member of the EU and that, in some sense, it represents an unexpected and unwelcome – albeit temporary – detour from the predestined stage of post-traditional modernity.

The question posed by Antal Örkény, the author of this study, was, why did 'ethnic origin, common descent, and shared religious belief define the new Hungarian identity, instead of the intellectual achievements, economic successes, common interests, or guaranteed civic rights'?[28] His answer throws light on the divergent attitudes of the EU technocracy and Hungarian public culture towards this question. Örkény noted that after the regime change in Hungary, 'for the first time in history' this nation 'possessed all the requisites that were considered essential for national independence by classics of nationalistic thought'. In previous times, Hungary could not take for granted its national independence, and therefore many of its people regard their national identity as a precious asset that was well worth preserving. Unlike most of Western Europe, Hungary did not go through the stage of enjoying genuine national independence in the nineteenth century, and therefore lacked the institutional foundation through which it could cultivate its national identity. Örkény stated that in an important sense, 'Hungary, like other nations of Eastern Europe, had caught up with late nineteenth-century Western Europe', and 'consequently, the historical gap between Western Europe and Eastern Europe had not narrowed'.[29]

In other words, the uneven pattern of development of national identity has led to a divergence between nations that could take their identity for granted and those who have struggled to reappropriate the consciousness of nationality that was silenced during the communist era.

Throughout most of its history, Hungary had a troublesome and insecure relationship with its national identity. Prior to this country's integration into the Soviet bloc, there were interminable discussions on what it meant to be Magyar. A collection of essays titled *What is a Magyar* published in 1939 under the editorship of Gyula Szekfü attempted to find a way of establishing what constituted the Hungarian character. However, as with all attempts to come to terms with this subject, there was little agreement amongst contributors to this collection.[30] During the Soviet era in Hungary, the question of Hungarian national identity could not be openly and seriously explored.

Nor was this issue directly addressed during the roundtable negotiations that lead to regime change in Hungary in 1989. During the transition from the Soviet-dominated era to that of national independence, the question of what it means to be Hungarian was left in abeyance. In particular, the relation of the newly emerging Hungarian democratic system to its historical past was explicitly ignored during the negotiations between the different political parties in the roundtable discussions. This reluctance to raise historical issues meant that even some of the defining moments of the nation's recent history, such as the 1956 Hungarian Revolution and the injustices committed by the post-1945 regimes, were more or less wilfully overlooked.

For a significant section of Hungarian society and its political leaders, regime change did not provide the nation with a distinct identity. For many, especially those of nationalist inclination, the absence of a new Constitution served as a reminder of the incomplete character of transition.[31] From their perspective, a genuine break from the Soviet era required the cultivation of an identity that positively reflected the hitherto un-discussed and un-acknowledged national character of the Hungarian people. That is why from 1989 onwards, the meaning of 'Hungarianness' became yet again a subject of debate.[32]

It is not surprising that since 1989, Hungarian public life often appears to be drawn towards an exploration of its past tradition. During the era of Soviet domination, the people of Hungary, like those of East Europe, were discouraged from exploring their national identity. Hungary's national traditions were treated as a sensitive subject and open expressions of national sentiments were actively frowned upon. In such circumstances, people felt inhibited about publicly discussing their attitudes towards their nation's past or even how they identified themselves. Official state doctrine actively discouraged the adoption of a distinct Hungarian identity.

Of course, even during the communist era, the interest in Hungarian identity and Hungary's place in the world could not be entirely extinguished. For example, a collection of essays titled *Our Place In Europe* (1986) sought to engage with this interest by providing a variety of views on this subject that were published during the twentieth century.[33] However, this was a very safe and risk-averse text that self-consciously sought to avoid controversy and one which treated the question of what it meant to be a Hungarian as a problem that was dealt with and resolved in the past. The issue was further avoided by focusing on the old question debated in the nineteenth and first half of the twentieth centuries of whether Hungary belonged to East, Central, or Western Europe. In this way the normative problem of tradition and identity was recast as a geographical issue of Hungary's place in the world.

For many Hungarians the establishment of an independent nation free from the yoke of Soviet domination stimulated an interest in the traditions of the pre-1945 past. The very fact that this past was one that was frequently condemned by the discredited Stalinist regime encouraged a section of the public to look to it to validate their identity. Hostility to Hungary's communist past was often paralleled by the adoption of an interest in the past that pre-dated it. For many Hungarians, this was a past that was, until recently, hidden from their view.

Political parties that were linked to the old communist regime and their allies were reluctant to dwell on Hungary's past because, like their counterparts in Western Europe, they regarded national sentiments and traditions as inherently dangerous and potentially volatile. At the same time, they were aware that nationalist sentiments and symbols continued to exercise a powerful influence over the outlook of the Hungarian electorate. Before his election as the socialist prime minister of Hungary in 1994, Gyula Horn, formerly a leading member of the old communist government and then head of the Socialist Party, told an interviewer that 'I consider all matters "national"', and added that 'our national consciousness has its traditions'. He recalled that this was a tradition with strong links with the history of the Hungarian left. 'The populist-national trend in Hungary, so often mentioned these days, started on the Left, and its values, aims even its representatives were leftists,' argued Horn.[34]

Horn's attempt to reclaim the legacy of populist nationalism for the left represented a pragmatic attempt to associate his party with Hungary's national sentiment. However, by the time that Parliament debated the proposal in 1999 that led to the *Lex Millenaris* – the Millennium Law – the parties of the left were at a loss as to know how to relate to nationalist sentiment. The debate on the law, which incorporated the Crown of Saint Stephen as the symbol of the nation, unleashed fundamental differences of opinion towards the nation's past.

The Law, which was the first of the new millennium – Act. I./2000 – represented an explicit attempt to provide a legal expression to Hungary's historical continuity. At the time the Socialist Party (MSZP) and the Alliance of Free Democrats (SZDSZ) opposed the calls to endow the Crown with legal significance on the grounds that, despite being a national treasure, it was an outdated relic.[35] However, once it became evident that the law would pass and that it enjoyed popular support, opposition became more muted. Instead of explicitly opposing the enactment of Saint Stephen's Crown, those hostile to it opted to minimize the law's status by arguing that it possessed only a symbolic significance. However, what the debate surrounding the Crown indicated was that this symbol could help to legitimate the Hungarian state by providing it with a sense of historical continuity.

Concern and anxiety with the wording of the Act. I./2000 amongst anti-traditionalists was intensified by the realization that the Hungarian public reacted positively to it and was drawn towards the sense of tradition and historical continuity. The symbolic and cultural authority of the Crown represents the antithesis of precisely the values – identities detached from national history – celebrated by Habermas.[36] For the anti-traditionalists, unable to relate to the national sentiments held by millions of people, the Crown merely symbolized a dark and ominous past.

This outlook was articulated in a lecture given at Cornell University by Hungary's permanent critic, Kim Scheppele. She stated that the interpretation and meaning attached to the Crown is 'fraught with toxicity from a progressive perspective'. However despite its supposed toxicity, Schepelle could not bring herself to simply denounce Saint Stephen's Crown. A report on this lecture indicated that Scheppele argued that 'the Crown is too deeply embedded in the hearts of Hungarians to let conservative interpretations of it go unanswered'. Apparently her 'project' was to develop the argument that the Crown was embedded in a 'far more progressive tradition than is traditionally understood'.[37]

Yet the very idea of inscribing the Crown within a new, allegedly different tradition is likely to unravel, so long as its advocates regard the very idea of tradition as toxic. Alternative new traditions that are invented instrumentally lack the moral depth required to motivate or inspire. There are of course a number of competing versions of Hungarian history and of the historical significance of Saint Stephen's Crown. But what gives the Crown its symbolic influence is not a particular narrative of the past: it is its capacity to offer a meaningful sense of continuity to people's quest for identity. That is precisely what the law enshrining its symbolic status attempted to achieve.

The revival of public interest in the Crown caught many Hungarian intellectuals and commentators unawares. From their standpoint it was the association of the Crown with the historical past that condemned it as totally irrelevant to the needs of the twenty-first century. As Lászlo Péter wrote in his study 'The Holy Crown of Hungary':

> it was generally taken for granted, even by opponents of the Communist regime, that political traditions, like the ideas of the Holy Crown, however important they had been in past centuries, were closely tied to the institution of the monarchy that had irretrievably perished by the end of the Second World War.[38]

Commenting on the unexpected re-emergence of the Crown as a symbol of Hungarian identity, Péter writes how the 'Holy Crown, like that fabled Egyptian bird, the phoenix, miraculously came forth with new life'.[39] Public acceptance of traditional historic symbols, which many thought were curiosities of interest to museums and collectors of antiques, showed that the question of the nation's tradition retained its salience for public life.

Hungarian opponents of the restoration of the Crown tradition regarded the ceremony surrounding its enactment as a meaningless performance. Balázs Trencsényi was scathing about what he described as these 'pompous celebrations'.[40] Nevertheless, even this critic acknowledged that this attempt to re-invent an old tradition constituted a response to an evident problem of legitimacy of the newly emerged Hungarian state. Trencsényi observed that the institutions of the post-communist Hungarian state had 'limited historical referentiality', and their relationship with the public lacked moral depth and meaning. In other words, the immediate post-communist Hungarian state had only a tangential relationship to the nation's past and could not draw on historical experience to validate itself. Trencsényi wrote that 'this framework turned out to be unable to provide mass support for the government', which is why, he claimed, 'Orbán and the intellectual circle around him opted for a more history-centred strategy of legitimization'.[41]

The controversy surrounding the status of Saint Stephen's Crown, and more generally of the role of tradition, was implicitly a debate about how the legitimacy of a state and its institutions are constituted. This problem of legitimacy is one of the fundamental issues confronting public life – and not just in Hungary, since ultimately it highlights the question of what constitutes the foundation for the authority of the state.

The problem of foundation

Throughout history, the foundation on which authority has rested has been subject to variation. At times the source of authority was located in religion, or tradition and custom, or popular sovereignty, or science, or in the persona of a charismatic leader, or in legal rules and procedures. The political theorist Hannah Arendt, in her excellent essay 'What is Authority?', took the view that historically, tradition, religion, and authority were mutually reinforcing institutions, and of these tradition 'has proved to be the most stable element'.[42] Her essay suggests that attempts to displace tradition with an alternative source of legitimation, such as science or legal rules, lack the moral and normative foundation necessary for accomplishing this task.

The relevance of Arendt's insight was strikingly confirmed by the experience of Hungary, where the institutionalization of the post-communist regime lacked a normative foundation and the cultural resources to enjoy legitimacy amongst the public. The post-communist transition paradigm, which was underpinned by the acceptance of European institutional practices and liberal-democratic procedural rules, provided a consensus that could be accepted by the different factions of the political elite. However, respect for this new paradigm and for its procedural rules simply signalled acceptance of the rules of the game. It did not provide the state with the normative foundation on which its authority could rest.

To a significant extent, the legitimacy of the new regime rested on its relationship to Europe and its association with the historical triumph of Western capitalism over Soviet communism. What the regime lacked was normative foundation, which, as I discuss elsewhere, constitutes the *problem of foundation*.[43] Historical experience indicates that newly enacted rules, procedures, and laws possess no intrinsic authority.

The legal scholar Harold Berman explains that 'in all societies', the law 'derives its authority from something outside itself'. That 'something' which is separate from, and logically prior to, the formulation of a rule or the codification of a law is the *source* or the *foundation* of its authority. The issue of normative foundation is particularly significant in the aftermath of a serious political transition such as that of the regime change in Hungary. When 'a legal system undergoes rapid change,' notes Berman, 'questions are inevitably raised concerning the legitimacy of the sources of its authority'.[44]

Regime change in Hungary occurred under conditions that avoided debate on what constituted the normative foundation of the new regime. Though an engagement with this issue could be postponed, it could not be avoided indefinitely. As it turned out, the gradual erosion of the transition consensus took the form of a clash of values about the meaning of Hungarian identity and the relationship of the nation to its historical past. Trencsényi argues that this *Kulturkampf* was 'linked to the reactualization of the interwar conflict of populists and urbanites, which, after 1989, was often reduced to a clash of "ethno-nationalists" and "cosmopolites"'.[45]

This observation fails to recognize that there was an essential difference between the interwar and the post-1989 debate. The early debate was one in which, despite fundamental differences, all sides recognized that questions such as Hungary's place in the world and the meaning of Hungarian identity were important to address.[46] In contrast, in the post-communist era, the anti-traditionalist political protagonists in this drama sought to avoid a debate that drew on the experience of the past.

Since 1989, anti-traditionalist intellectuals and politicians have attempted to avoid a debate about the past by arguing that it represents a diversion from present-day problems. While dwelling on the past can certainly be used as a tactic of diversion, reason for condemning it in this instance was often caused by a reluctance or inability to give meaning to national sentiment. From this standpoint, attachment to national tradition was perceived as a disturbing character fault. For example, the Hungarian journalist, János Széky, wrote of the 'Curse of Continuity' in reaction to the fact that the 'Hungarian nation-state has a singularly strong and continuous pre-communist political tradition'. Why? Because this tradition was 'essentially undemocratic' and did not provide the political left with a legacy that it could draw on. Thus, Széky decried Hungary's political traditions because they provided right-wing politicians with an unfair advantage over their left-wing opponents. He wrote that 'Fidesz, which emerged as the dominant right-wing party in the late 1990s, consciously built up an image of the "great Hungarian past" out of second-hand fragments of pre-1944 ideology, while there was very little that left-wingers and liberals could set against the emotionally powerful, history-based nationalist agitation'.[47]

That Hungarian 'left-wingers and liberals' were at a loss to know how to engage in a battle of values over the nation's historical legacy was in part influenced by their constant underestimation of its importance for addressing the problem of state legitimacy. Széky's use of the term the 'Curse of Continuity' signalled a preference for the presentist historiography favoured by academic partisans of European federalism. What can best be characterized as the Year Zero history promoted by the EU is a history of discontinuity between the past before 1945 and afterwards.[48] Such history celebrates the achievements of the EU since 1945 while discreetly freeing itself from the legacy of the bad old days before 1945. Such a history begged the question, what was the relation between a nation and its past? It self-consciously avoided working out the historical legacy on which the post-1989 Hungarian state could draw.

Year Zero history is symptomatic of the trend of 'hiding the values of the past' by EU leaders that we discussed in the previous chapter. Historical continuity may be a curse, but without the legitimacy offered by a meaningful legacy, the exercise of political authority will invariably be called into question. There are no examples of successful political systems that could entirely bypass establishing a relationship with a tradition that possesses some meaning to their citizens. Hannah Arendt's discussion of the successful founding of the United States is pertinent in this respect.

Arendt noted how the Preamble of the American Declaration of Independence contains an appeal to 'nature's God', 'which relates to transcendent source of authority for the laws of the new body politic'. In this respect Thomas Jefferson's famous words 'We hold these truths to be self-evident' clearly gives voice to a truth that is not a product of reasoning. It is a truth that is beyond debate and discussion. Agreement is with a truth 'that needs no agreement since, because of its self-evidence, it compels without argumentative demonstration of personal persuasion'.[49] Such a powerful assertion of truths that are beyond discussion required at least an implicit agreement on the traditions that underwrote the American way of life.

While the eighteenth century American Constitution was successful in providing a solution to the problem of normative foundation, there are very few truths left in contemporary Europe that are held to be 'self-evident'. That is why supporters of the enactment of the Crown of Saint Stephen opted to spell out, at length, a story of foundation for the Hungarian state. A key passage from the Act 1/2000 states:

> One thousand years ago, the coronation of St István united the Hungarian people in a Christian faith to the rest of the European people. Hungary has been an integral part of Europe ever since. This has ensured the survival of Hungarians and their decisive role throughout the centuries. Hungary is still based on St István's state founding work.

The act also claimed that in 'national consciousness and in the tradition of Hungarian common law, the Holy Crown lives on as a relic manifesting the continuity and independence of the Hungarian state'[50]

Whether the enactment of the Crown and related rituals designed to both revive and invent a sense of tradition succeeds in capturing the Hungarian public's imagination remains to be seen. But this attempt at a very public affirmation of historical continuity and traditions at least attempts to deal with the problem of foundation. It stands in sharp contrast to hiding the values of the past.

Tradition and authority

The controversy that has surrounded relations between Hungary and the EU in recent years is not simply due to differences over policy and procedure. They are underpinned by a clash of values. They are also fuelled by a very different appreciation of historical continuities and the role of tradition. As noted previously, the approach of the EU on these matters is most coherently expressed by Jürgen Habermas, whose critique of historical continuity and of tradition is founded on the premise that these supposedly irrational influences inevitably lead to xenophobia and racial conflict.

The current fashionable critique of tradition is based on a uniquely fatalistic teleology of gloom that regards the Holocaust as the inexorable consequence of the political appeal of national traditions and historical continuities. However, this argument is essentially an updated version of earlier and more mainstream criticisms of tradition. Such criticisms have their roots in the eighteenth-century Age of Reason, when science, rationality, and enlightenment were portrayed as the polar opposite to tradition. This attitude was frequently displayed by the French *philosophes*. In his *Encyclopédie*, Diderot celebrated 'trampling on prejudice, tradition, universal consent, authority' since he believed that these values enslaved people's minds.

The arguments of the *philosophes* emphasized the irrational, mystical, and anti-modern features of traditional values. In their more extreme version, such arguments made no attempt to distinguish between values that were demeaning or harmful and those that possessed virtue. They were all rejected because they were old traditions.

These sentiments gained ascendancy in Western societies in the twentieth century, and a long time before the Holocaust, European elite culture became increasingly distanced from the values of tradition. The appropriation of the Holocaust into the armoury of anti-traditional arguments was designed to enhance the legitimacy of sentiments that have long pre-dated this tragedy.

In his study *Tradition and Authority* (1972), Carl Joachim Friedrich, the German-American political theorist, drew attention to the tendency to treat tradition as a form of misleading prejudice.[51] Unlike many of his colleagues, Friedrich sought to rescue and reinvigorate tradition as a concept that was relevant for modern times. In particular, he insisted that tradition is not 'unrelated to reason and reasoning' and that 'tradition is often the very basis of reasoning and rational argument'. Friedrich claimed that tradition was only a problem if it was promoted as an end in itself; he argued that 'too much tradition ossifies a political order, but equally surely, too little tradition undermines and dissolves the community and its order'.[52] Friedrich contrasted the concept of tradition to that of traditionalism. He asserted that traditionalism was the 'self-conscious and deliberate insistence upon the value of tradition' that attempted to make it 'a norm of behaviour' and warned that if carried too far, it would become an ideology.[53] Friedrich sought to provide an argument for getting the balance right between the relying on the experience of the past and the use of reasoning in the present.

In her writings on the modern condition, Arendt was concerned with what she perceived as the declining influence of tradition. She understood that the influence of tradition and its values on modern society were likely to become marginalized. Though she was concerned about the erosion of tradition, she insisted that the consequences of this process were not entirely negative. She wrote that: 'with the loss of tradition we have lost the thread which safely guided us through the vast realms of the past, but this thread was also the chain fettering each successive generation to a predetermined aspect of the past.'[54] Arendt suggested that the loss of this 'thread' could have some positive outcomes: 'It could be that only now will the past open up to us with unexpected freshness and tell us things no one has yet had ears to hear.'[55] In other words, the loss of a particular tradition could help society to look back upon the past with 'unexpected freshness' and rediscover experience and traditions that were obscured by the more recent traditions that dominated its view of the world.

Despite the advantage of freeing the younger generations from the chain linking them to the past, Arendt seems to suggest that the damage that such a complete break from tradition could cause outweighs its benefits. She argued that 'it cannot be denied that without a securely anchored tradition – and the loss of this security occurred several hundred years ago – the whole dimension of the past has also been endangered.' In particular, she feared that humanity could deprive itself of 'one dimension, the dimension of depth in human existence'. For Arendt such depth was inextricably linked with the capacity to reflect on and engage with the meanings of the past. She reminds us that 'memory and depth are the same' and that 'depth cannot be reached by man except through remembrance'.[56]

The dimension of depth in human existence touches on the realm of meaning and of values. That is why in some form or another, genuine authority needs to draw upon the legacy and experience of tradition and the past. Like Arendt, the German sociologist Max Weber understood that in the modern world the influence of tradition had declined and could not be expected to provide the foundation for authority. To explore and explain this development Weber worked out his influential typology of the grounds on which legitimate authority was based:

> **Rational grounds**, grounded on belief in the validity of legal rules issued through legal authority.
> **Traditional grounds**, based on long-standing beliefs in the 'sanctity of immemorial traditions' and customs and which endows traditional authority with legitimacy.
> **Charismatic grounds**, based on the popular acclaim and loyalty to the 'exceptional sanctity, heroism or exemplary character of an individual person, expressed through charismatic authority'.[57]

Numerous social theorists have questioned the utility of this typology on the grounds that it draws too direct a contrast between the rational/legal and the traditional grounds for constructing legitimacy. What is said to be rational may be the outcome of a priori subjective preference and what is characterized as traditional may well be the product of previous reasoning. Friedrich has criticized the typology for drawing a direct contrast between traditional and rational-legal authority, taking particular issue with the tendency to represent tradition as irrational and the rational-legal as its opposite.[58]

Weber posited a model that claimed that the rationalization of social life would lead to the ascendancy of authority based on rational grounds. However, this displacement of traditional reasoning by instrumental attitudes raised the question of what was the normative foundation of the technical rules linked with rational-legal authority. As the experience of the EU and of the immediate post-1989 Hungarian government indicated, legal and bureaucratic rules need a normative foundation if authority is to have real meaning. Impersonal rules on their own are unlikely to provide the foundation for authoritative action.

What values?

Max Weber was aware of the limited potential that legal-rational rules have to inspire belief in the legitimacy of the political order. Indeed, one reason why Weber became so interested in the problem of authority was because he could not convince himself that with the decline of tradition, the modern state could draw on a new source of foundational authority.

Experience suggests that Weber's concept of legal-rational legitimacy provides a relatively fragile foundation for authorizing political rule. As one of Weber's critics wrote: he had 'great difficulties in pinning legal legitimacy down to beliefs and normative compliance, partly because procedural regularities in legal-decision making do not provide a satisfactory alternative to substantive justice and natural law'.[59] The rational-legal lacks the cultural and moral resources possessed by tradition to motivate and influence the public. As one legal sociologist observed, the law is 'rather cold and bloodless' and 'cannot replace traditional authority in the expressive, emotional sense'. He added that it 'is possible to worship the idea of law; but law does not hold authority in the modern world because of its grip on the emotions'.[60] Weber was all too aware of the limited capacity of rational-legal norms to inspire the public. 'Compared with firm beliefs in the positive religiously revealed character of a legal norm or in the inviolable sacredness of an age-old tradition, even the most convincing norms arrived at by abstraction seem to be too subtle to serve as the bases of a legal system,' he wrote.[61]

Moreover the law itself needs to draw on cultural resources external to itself to render it not just valid but morally compelling. As the social theorist David Beetham argued, there are 'substantive and moral questions about the content and justification of law itself'.[62] He has gone as far as to claim that the failure to 'provide any account at all of the normative (as opposed to the juridical) legitimation of the law' actually 'invalidates Weber's account of legitimacy'.[63]

Without any moral or normative content, it is far from evident how belief in rules and procedures gives meaning to authority. The political scientist Robert Grafstein stated that 'belief in legality amounts to an empty verbal resolution of the substantive problem of accounting for obedience under conditions of diversity'. He added that 'Weber simply fails to establish an adequate motivational basis for submitting to varied decisions that are grounded by their mode of genesis rather than their content'.[64] The legal scholar Lawrence Friedman echoed a similar point. He concluded that the displacement of traditional forms by rational-legal authority created a problem since the law is 'a limited authority'.[65] In other words, legal-rational authority does not possess equivalent influence to that of the authority of tradition. Something more than just legal rules are needed for the constitution of authority.

The debate in the European Parliament in January 2012 was ultimately grounded on two very different conceptions regarding the normative foundations of political authority. In this debate, the European Parliament's opponents of the Hungarian Constitution were not simply reacting to the specific clauses of the document. They intuitively understood that a constitution founded on an appeal to the traditions of the past directly contradicted the EU's project of developing a form of transnational authority based on respect for rules and procedures.

Jürgen Habermas has consistently pointed to the contradiction between legitimacy based on the normative foundation of tradition and one based on the law. His objective is the establishment of a form of political authority that relies upon a democratically 'juridified decision-making and administrative power'. Habermas' attachment to the EU project is, in part, linked to his belief that transnational institutions tend to transform political issues into juridical ones, thereby reducing the necessity for legitimating the authority of the political. His ultimate objective is a world Parliament where decisions are 'monitored by courts'. Habermas' attempt to liberate authority from any direct relationship to a national constituency and national traditions lead to a world that is managed by an alliance of enlightened technocrats and courts. He noted that a 'fortunate consequence of the restriction to legal but fundamentally moral matters is a deflation of the demands on legitimation of the world organization'.[66]

If the experience of the EU is anything to go, the strategy of seeking to deflate 'demands on legitimation' through policies of technocratic juridification is unlikely to prove effective. In particular, the issue of legitimation cannot be suppressed once political disputes assume the form of conflict over values. As François Foret and Annabelle Littoz-Monnet argue, 'the specific nature of value-based controversies calls into question traditional legitimation mechanisms of EU-level governance'.[67] Foret and Littoz-Monnet point out that the institutions of the EU, which tend to rely on the authority of the expert regulator, find it difficult to respond to values-led challenges to its legitimacy.

With the best will in the world, the reference to Christianity and values associated with Hungary's national traditions in the Fundamental Law would be perceived as a provocation by politicians wedded to a style of governance based on expert-oriented mechanisms of legitimation. That the EU oligarchy is uncomfortable with values and almost instinctively seeks to bury them is the direct outcome of its own insecure sense of legitimacy. Foret and Littoz-Monnet note:

> Because EU policy-making was long perceived as essentially regulatory in nature, expertise was accepted as a central justification and legitimation mechanism for

policy choices. The rise of value-based controversies has thrown into question the EU's output centered legitimation strategies. Both the public and academic commentators have become critical of exclusive reliance on expertise as a means of escaping ordinary means of public accountability.[68]

It is the recognition that the claim to expert authority is insufficient to legitimate the EU that has fuelled the acrimony towards populist movements that raise questions about its values. Expert authority regards populist values – particularly the avowal of popular sovereignty – as a direct threat to its authority.

Since the 2012 European Parliamentary debate on Hungary, disputes about values have become far more prevalent, and the EU has found it difficult to develop a mechanism for reconciling different versions or interpretations of European values. It is far easier to resolve arguments over economic resources or political reforms than disputes over cultural values. Since values touch on the meaning of life and first principles, those committed to a different outlook often find that they express themselves in a language that is incomprehensible to others. A lot can get lost in translation in a debate on values. That is why, as Foret and Littoz-Monnet explained, 'the emergence of value-based controversies in EU politics raises specific problems in terms of conflict settlement mechanisms at the supranational level'. They observed that:

> Value-based controversies consist of debates over first principles, in which at least one advocacy coalition involved portrays the issue as one of morality and uses moral arguments in its policy advocacy. As a result, they do not lend themselves well to traditional negotiation mechanisms in supranational arenas, characterised by bargaining techniques such as issue linkages and trade-offs. Those might indeed be ineffective in issues where values are perceived to be at stake. In situations where a clash of values is present, reaching a policy compromise is highly unlikely. Thus, the presence of values in EU politics poses new problems related to the management of diversity, when differences are too insurmountable.[69]

In recent years, the Culture Wars have become internationalized, and disputes about lifestyle, family life, sexual orientation, or the nature of community life are no longer confined to the domestic sphere. In Europe as well as internationally, culture has become politicized around issues such as the role of multiculturalism, mass migration into the continent, the nature of borders, the challenge posed by radical Islamists groups, the nature of marriage and family life, and sexuality. Muslim jihadists are not just fighting with bombs: they are directly questioning Western liberal values and denouncing them as immoral. Radical Muslim websites condemn the West for its materialism, consumerism, and sinful behaviour. In turn, supporters of Western post-traditional values criticize societies in the Middle East for the way they treat women and homosexuals. Even Russia has been pulled into the frame, frequently denounced by Western commentators for its conservative and traditional attitude towards women and homosexuality.

In response to the anti-traditionalist values celebrated in the United States and the West, Vladamir Putin, the President of Russia, has sought to assume the posture of the global leader fighting for traditionalism and a Christian way of life. There is little doubt that the government of Russia is a willing participant in what it regards as a war over moral values and beliefs. Since early 2012 President Putin has explicitly expressed his conviction that 'cultural self-awareness, spiritual and moral values, codes of values are an area of intense competition'. Putin has stated that the struggle 'to influence the worldviews of entire ethnic groups, the desire to subject them to one's will, to force one's system of values and beliefs upon them is an absolute reality, just like the fight for mineral resources that many nations, ours included experience'.[70]

Vladimir Putin self-consciously cultivates the image of Russia as a moral crusader fighting for the survival of human civilization. In his annual State of the Nation speech in 2013, Putin responded to Western criticisms of Russia's attitude to homosexuality by lamenting the decline of morality in the West, and drawing attention to what he perceived as the morally disorienting consequences of Western social engineering. 'This destruction of traditional values from above not only entails negative consequences for society, but is also inherently anti-democratic because it is based on an abstract notion and runs counter to the will of the majority of people,' he claimed, arguing that traditional family values were the only effective defence against 'so-called tolerance – genderless and infertile'.

Although directed at the Russian public, Putin's denunciation of 'genderless and infertile' lifestyles was also messaged for a global audience. Just a few days before the delivery of this speech, an influential Kremlin-linked think-tank published a report titled 'Putin: World Conservatism's New Leader'. The report claimed that ordinary people throughout the world yearn for the stability and security offered by traditional values and argued that people believe in the traditional family and regard multiculturalism with suspicion. Dmitry Abzalov, a spokesman, told the press that 'it is important for most people to preserve their way of life, their lifestyle, their traditions' and because of that they 'tend toward conservatism'.[71]

It is not yet clear whether Moscow's celebration of conservative traditional values will amount to more than an exercise in state propaganda. But regardless of the consequences, this demonstrates that even in the twenty-first century, tradition and the values associated with the past continue both to inspire and repel. The conflict between the federalist minded leaders of the EU and the Orbán government reflects in miniature the growing tendency for international disputes to assume a cultural form.

Notes

1 See for example Ben-Ami, S. (2016) 'Populism, Past and Present', *Project Syndicate*, 10 August 2016, www.project-syndicate.org/commentary/populism-economic-grievances-by-shlomo-ben-ami-2016-08?barrier=accessreg.
2 Rogoziv, L. (2017) 'Liberal vs Illiberal: Welcome to the New Bipolar World', *The Moscow Times*, 7 February 2017, https://themoscowtimes.com/articles/liberal-vs-illiberal-welcome-to-the-new-bipolar-world-57068.

3 See account of his lecture in Budapest – https://444.hu/2014/05/29/habermas-magyarorszag-tavolabb-kerult-europatol/.

4 Delanty, G. (1996) 'Habermas and Post-National Identity: Theoretical Perspectives on the Conflict in Northern Ireland', *Irish Political Studies*, vol. 11, no. 1, pp. 21–22.

5 See Habermas, J. (1988) 'Historical Consciousness and Post-Traditional Identity: Remarks on the Federal Republic's Orientation to the West Author(s): Jürgen Habermas Source', *Acta Sociologica*, vol. 31, no. 1, pp. 3–13.

6 *ibid.*

7 Müller, J.-W. (2007) *Constitutional Patriotism*, Princeton University Press, Princeton, p. 29.

8 See Furedi (2013) Chapter 6, 'Medieval claim-making and the sociology of tradition' in Furedi (2013).

9 Shils, (1981) *Authority*, The University of Chicago Press: Chicago, p. 21.

10 Müller, J.-W. (2007) *Constitutional Patriotism*, Princeton University Press, Princeton, p. 33.

11 Arendt (1951).

12 Habermas (2016) *The Crisis of the European Union*, Polity: Cambridge, p. 45.

13 See Müller, J.-W. (2006) 'On the Origins of Constitutional Patriotism', *Contemporary Political Theory*, vol. 5, no. 3, pp. 287–288.

14 Scheppele (2000) p. 13.

15 Scheppele, K. L. (2000) 'Constitutional Basis of Hungarian Conservatism', *The Eastern European Constitutional Review*, vol. 9, p. 51.

16 See www.frankfuredi.com/site/article/599/

17 See Prins, G. & Salisbury, R. (2008) *Risk, Threat and Security: The Case of the United Kingdom*, www.lse.ac.uk/researchAndExpertise/units/mackinder/pdf/Prins%20and%20Salisbury.pdf.

18 See *The Washington Times* – November 21, 2016.

19 *ibid.*

20 Tonnies (1955) pp. 263–265.

21 Friedrich (1972) p. 33.

22 Habermas, J. (1998) 'Historical Consciousness and Post-Traditional Identity: Remarks on the Federal Republic's Orientation to the West', *Acta Sociologica*, vol. 31, no. 1, p. 7.

23 Klinke, I. (2014) 'European Integration Studies and the European Union's Eastern Gaze', *Millennium Journal of International Studies*, vol. 43, no.2, p. 572.

24 See Calligaro, O. (2013) *Negotiating Europe: The EU Promotion of Europeanness since the 1950s*, Basingstoke: Palgrave, p. 74.

25 Klinke (2014) pp. 478–479.

26 See Pänke, J. (2015) 'The Fallout of the EU's Normative Imperialism in the Eastern Neighborhood', *Problems of Post-Communism*, vol. 62, no. 6, pp. 350–363.

27 Örkény, A. (2005) 'Hungarian National Identity', *International Journal of Sociology*, vol. 35, no. 4, Winter 2005–6, p. 1.

28 *ibid*, p. 2.

29 *ibid*, p. 2.

30 See Szekfü, G. (1939) *Mi A Magyar?*, Magyar Szemle Társaság: Budapest.

31 On this point see Fowler, B. (2004) 'Nation, State, Europe and National Revival in Hungarian Party Politics: The Case of the Millennial Commemorations', *Europe-Asia Studies*, vol. 56, no. 1, p. 61.

32 See Deme, L. (1998) 'Perceptions and Problems of Hungarian Nationality and National Identity in the early 1990s', *International Journal of Politics, Culture and Society*, vol. 12, no. 2, pp. 309–310.

33 See Berend, T. I. (ed) (1986) *Helyünk Európába; Nézetek és koncpeciok a 20 századi Magyarországon*, vol. 2, Magvetö Kiadó: Budapest.

34 Cited in Deme (1998) p. 323, The title of the interview is "I Would Like to Know Why We are Not National!"

35 See the discussion in Paul Nemes 'Crown Fever'. www.ce-review.org/00/1/nemes1.html.

36 See Habermas (1998).

37 See, The Hungarian Crown, Occupy Wall Street, and the Politics of the Left, www. religiousleftlaw.com/2011/11/the-hungarian-crown-occupy-wall-street-and-the-politics-of-the-left.html.
38 Peter, L. (2003) 'The Holy Crown of Hungary, Visible and Invisible', *SEER*, vol. 81, no. 3, p. 422.
39 *ibid*.
40 Trencsényi, B. (2014) 'Beyond Liminality? The Kulturkampf of the Early 2000s in East Central Europe', *Boundary 2*, vol. 41, no. 1, p. 136.
41 *ibid*.
42 Arendt, H. (1954) *What Is Authority*, p. 2.
43 See Furedi, F. (2013) *Authority: A Sociological History*. Cambridge University Press: Cambridge.
44 Berman (1983) p. 16.
45 Trencsényi (2014) p. 136.
46 See for example the collection of essays – Szekfű Gyula (ed) (1939) *Mi a magyar?* Magyar Szemle Társaság, Budapest. See also works by Jászi Oskár and Bibo István.
47 See Széky, J. (2014) 'A Tradition of Nationalism: The Case of Hungary', *Eurozine*, www. eurozine.com/articles/2014-04-11-szeky-en.html.
48 On Year Zero History see chapter 'the Politics of Memory'.
49 Arendt (2006) p. 184.
50 Kovács, M. (2014) *Magyars and Political Discourses in the New Millennium: Changing Meanings in Hungary at the Start of the Twenty-First Century*, Lexington Books, Lanham, MD.
51 Friedrich (1972) p. 33.
52 Friedrich (1972) p. 14.
53 Friedrich (1972) p. 18.
54 Arendt (2006) p. 94.
55 Arendt (2006) p. 94.
56 Arendt (2006) p. 94.
57 Weber (1978) p. 215.
58 Friedrich (1972) p. 33.
59 Turner (1992) p. 200.
60 Friedman (1994) pp. 118 & 112.
61 Weber (1978) p. 874.
62 Beetham (1991b) p. 5.
63 Beetham (1991a) p. 40.
64 Grafstein (1981) p. 468.
65 Friedman (1994) p. 53.
66 Habermas (2016) pp. 9 & 65.
67 Foret, F. & Littoz-Monnet, A. (2014) 'Legitimisation and Regulation of and through Values', *Politique européenne*, no. 45, p. 16.
68 *ibid*.
69 *ibid*.
70 Cited in Robinson, N. 'The Political Origins of Russia's Culture Wars', www.academia. edu/6902059/The_Political_Origins_of_Russias_Culture_Wars.
71 See www.rferl.org/content/vladimir-ilyich-putin-the-conservative-lenin/25206293.html.

3

NATIONAL CONSCIOUSNESS VS DENATIONALIZED IDENTITY

Conflicts over values and traditions run in parallel with competing conceptions about the nature of authority and identity. As has been widely noted, since the rise of modernity, such differences have been often expressed through the contrast drawn between religious and secular values. In more recent times the contestation of authority is frequently focused on the nation. The anti-populist cultural script frames national sentiment as an outdated, dangerous, and irrational prejudice. This representation of nationalist consciousness has gained widespread traction in elite culture, where it tends to be derided as the bigotry of ordinary people. Anti-populist ideology continually signals the idea that if awakened, this narrow-minded sensibility will have harmful consequences.

In contemporary Western political discourse, nationalism, and its cognate terms – national attachments, national identity, national sentiments – have acquired the kind of negative qualities that usually invite moral condemnation. One of the criticisms mounted against Hungary is that this society has not moved with the times and is disoriented by its continued adherence to national attachments. Indeed the claim that Hungarian nationalism possesses uniquely disturbing psychological features serves to validate what I characterize as the theory of Hungarian exceptionalism.

Moral devaluation of nationhood

Since Carlton J. H. Hayes' influential essay 'Nationalism as a Religion' (1926), there has been a discernible tendency in the academic literature to treat nationalism as the irrational functional equivalent of religion. Often, nationalism is associated with atavistic, mystical, and emotional properties that have the capacity to disrupt the prevailing order. Hayes claimed that this secular religion possesses great emotional influence over the masses and noted that 'an emotional loyalty to the idea or the fact of the national state' was one that was 'so intensely emotional that it motivates all sorts of people and causes them to subordinate all other loyalties to national loyalty'.[1] Hayes' essay, which expressed the reaction of the liberal intelligentsia to the devastating consequences of the First World War, indicted nationalists as 'either ignorant and prejudiced or inhuman or jaundiced'. He added that nationalism was 'artificial' and was 'far from ennobling', describing it as *patriotic snobbery*.[2]

Writing in the 1930s, John Hobson summed up this outlook, when he warned of the 'chief perils and disturbances associated with the aggressive nationalism of today'.[3] Hobson's condemnation of 'aggressive nationalism' coexisted with the recognition that there could be non-aggressive or 'healthy' nationalisms. In the 1940s and 1950s, many liberal theorists wrote approvingly of the English variety, while deploring others. Hans Kohn's classic text of the 1940s praised Western nationalism as one that adhered to a basically 'rational and universal concept of political liberty and looked towards the city of the future'.[4] He drew a sharp contrast between rational nationalism and Eastern nationalism, which he claimed was 'basically founded on history, monuments, on graveyards, even harking back to the mysteries of ancient times and tribal solidarity'.[5]

The rise of Nazi aggression, the catastrophe of the Second World War, and the Holocaust are often perceived as the inevitable consequence of nationalist rivalries and ideologies. From this standpoint, national attachments are interpreted as a cultural resource that is dangerous because they can be mobilized to promote exclusionary and racial causes. That is why, in practice, the classical distinctions drawn between patriotism, identification with the nation and republican, civic, cultural, religious, and racial nationalism has lost some of its force. According to this teleological conception of nationalism, what at first appears as an innocent manifestation of national identity and loyalty in the nineteenth century inevitably crystallized into menacing political ideology, of which Nazism is the most barbaric manifestation.

Nationalism is almost single-handedly blamed for the catastrophe that engulfed the world between 1939 and 1945. The tendency to portray national attachments as not simply potentially dangerous but also as inherently a threat to global security gained momentum in the 1930s, and by the 1940s, it acquired the status of an incontrovertible truth. This sentiment was captured by a commentary published in *Foreign Affairs* in 1943, which observed that 'the word . . . [nationalism] . . . is now synonymous with the most vulgar racism'. It added that 'the work of this monster has culminated in two world wars and thirty million dead'.[6]

In the 1940s, some of the critics of nationalism still acknowledged that national sentiments and loyalties were not intrinsically harmful. In 1944, Frederick Herz wrote in his *Nationality in History and Politics* that 'few people would condemn nationalism outright', adding that 'English usage identifies it with national sentiment and the complete elimination of this sentiment would be widely deplored and resisted'.[7] Herz was deeply troubled by the phenomenon of nationalism and remarked that it was 'no longer possible to state' where 'the line of demarcation between beneficial and harmful nationalism is'.[8] However, the willingness shown by Herz to portray national sentiment as least a neutral, if not always positive, force, gradually gave way to a more negative assessment of this feeling.

By the 1960s many accounts of the topic of nationalism treated it as an unwelcome irrational pathology. Some theorists called into question the very essence of nationalism and national sentiments and portrayed those who still held onto such prejudices as lower forms of human beings. In his book, *Nationalism and Its Alternatives*, the Czech American political theorist Karl Deutsch could barely hide his contempt for those who hold national sentiments. 'A nation so goes a rueful European saying', he wrote, 'is a group of persons united by a common error about their ancestry and a common dislike of their neighbour'.[9]

If Herz were writing in the twenty-first century, it is unlikely that he would make the statement that 'few people would condemn nationalism outright'. In the contemporary era, the very legitimacy of the nation state has been put to question. This sentiment acquired a dominant influence amongst the Western intelligentsia in the post-Second World War era. As Johanna Möhring and Gwythian Prins point out, 'for more than two intellectual generations, since 1945, there has been an ascendant narrative in international affairs which has represented the nation state as pathological in its very nature'.[10] Such sentiments led many supporters of the EU to regard national sentiments as an expression of primordial attachments, which by definition do not have a positive role to play in a modern society.

EU policymakers often give the impression that they believe that national loyalties constitute an outdated prejudice and prefer attachments that are directed at rules and legal principles. Their references to national loyalties imply that if these sentiments are held too strongly they will provide a cultural terrain where exclusionary tendencies are likely to flourish. From this perspective the Fundamental Law of Hungary, particularly its Avowal of National Faith, represents an unwelcome throwback to an irrational pre-modern past, and it is perceived as problematic not only for its coupling of 'national' with 'faith' but also for its unapologetic celebration of loyalty to the nation.

The preference of European federalist intellectuals for a denationalized form of civic identity is the polar opposite of the approach adopted by the authors of the Fundamental Law, who self-consciously uphold the ideal of loyalty to the nation. As this chapter outlines, conflicting views about the status of national values and identity underpin the cultural tension between Hungary and the leaders of the EU.

It is important to note that the hostility of liberals towards national loyalties is a relatively recent development. The emergence of the modern world and of liberal Enlightenment ideals coincided with the rise of nation states and national loyalty. In the aftermath of the French Revolution, its leaders adopted the language of nationalism. Loyalty was singled out as a value worthy of respect by the drafters of the Constitution of the First Republic of France in 1793. Indeed in both the American and the French Constitutions, the ideas of sovereignty, people, and the nation are indissolubly bound together. In France, the form through which the General Will came to be expressed was the nation. This principle was enshrined in the Constitution of 1791, which stated that 'sovereignty is one, indivisible, inalienable and imprescriptible', and 'belongs to the Nation; no one section of the people, no one individual can claim the right to exercise it'.[11] Article 3 of the 1789 *Declaration of the Rights of Man and of the Citizen* stated that the 'sources of all sovereignty resides essentially in the nation; no body, no individual can exercise authority that does not proceed from it in plain terms'.

This invocation of the nation as the source of all sovereign authority was paralleled by an outburst of enthusiasm for human liberty and individual rights. At least in the American and French context, it was the influence of liberal and humanitarian ideals that helped to strengthen the 'new principle that all sovereign authority emanates from the nation as a whole and that the central government is the only legitimate executor of that authority'.[12] Today it is the authority of this nation state – in both its liberal and conservative form – that has been increasingly contested. Academic cosmopolitan theorists, who regard their current historical crusade against nationalism as the historical equivalent of the struggle against religious superstition in the early modern era, most explicitly convey this view. 'Just as Christian theology had to be repressed at the start of the Modern Period in Europe, the political sphere of action must be opened up today anew by taming nationalist theology' advised one of the foremost exponents of cosmopolitanism, the German sociologist Ulrich Beck.[13]

Divergent paths

References to the nation state and nationalism by European policymakers and academics are inescapably influenced by their reaction to the negative experience of the Second World War. Post-nationalist commentators interpret this global catastrophe as an experience that finally, and irrevocably, morally negates the legitimacy of the sense of nationhood and of identities forged around national cultures. Such views gained widespread influence in Western Europe, but particularly in Germany, where the burden of guilt imposed on the public psyche has discouraged the cultivation of national identity.

Unease regarding cultural or political appeals to the authority of the nation is often justified on the grounds that such appeals threaten to undermine the influence of rational civic deliberation over public life. Critics of the nation state also claim that national sentiments contain an inherent tendency towards escalating into hostility and aggression towards those of other nationalities. In the post-Second World War era, such criticisms were not confined to liberal and left-wing critics of political nationalism but also endorsed by many European conservative and European Christian Democratic leaders.

Despite the traditional association of conservatism with national culture, many prominent Christian Democrats became wary of nationalism; in the aftermath of the Second World War, one of their immediate aims was to contain the long-standing national rivalry between France and Germany. From this perspective, some form of European unity was perceived as the antidote to the threat posed by a potential conflict between these two nations. In a speech at Zurich University in September 1946, Winston Churchill spoke about the 'tragedy of Europe', and argued that 'we must build a kind of United States of Europe'. For Churchill, the precondition for European unity was the forging of a 'partnership between France and Germany'.[14]

Churchill did not express any animosity against nationalism or the sense of nation-hood as such: his focus was on the elimination of national rivalry between two old enemies. A similar outlook was conveyed by the Schuman Declaration of 1950, which proposed the pooling of coal and steel production as 'a first step in the fed-eration of Europe', and stated that the 'coming together of the nations of Europe requires the elimination of the age-old opposition of France and Germany'.[15]

Although the early attempts to promote European unity were not explicitly directed against the integrity of the nation state, many of the advocates of European federalism were clearly disenchanted with, and suspicious of, the role of nationalist attachment. Though at this point in time the authority of the nation state was rarely questioned explicitly, the positive sentiments that surrounded the sense of nation-hood when it emerged in the nineteenth century had clearly lost much of their appeal in post-war Europe.

Leading Christian Democratic politicians – the French statesman Robert Schuman, the German Chancellor Konrad Adenauer, the Prime Minister of Italy, Alcide De Gasperi – played an important role in the building of institutions of European unity in the 1940s and 1950s. In part, their enthusiasm for European unity represented a reac-tion to what they perceived as the excesses of nationalism. As one study of this process observed:

> 'European Christian Democratic parties supported the integration of West-ern Europe as a means of rebuilding the economies of their countries in the aftermath of the war, ensuring more stable political systems and overcoming nationalism'.[16]

This reaction against nationalism was particularly influential in Germany, where the post-Second World War elite felt the need to distance themselves from this nation's past. Chancellor Konrad Adenauer took the view that the integration of Germany into Europe would assist his nation in this way, and after the end of the Second World War, the Christian Democratic Party (CDU) enthusiastically adopted the policy of European unification. As the German political scientist Ernst Haas noted, 'in leading circles of the CDU, the triptych of self-conscious anti-Nazism, Christian values, and dedication to European unity as a means of redemption for past German sins has played a crucial ideological role'.[17]

Some studies of the leading role assumed by Christian Democratic politicians in the project of European unification have gone so far as to argue that this movement was intrinsically hostile to the ideals represented by the nation state. The cosmopoli-tan political theorist Jan-Werner Müller claims that nationalism is 'one of Christian Democrats' prime ideological enemies', and that they, 'like Catholics, international-ists by nature – placed little value on the nation state'.[18] However, it was pragmatic calculations rather than any fundamental internationalist principle that led Chris-tian Democrats to adopt the cause of European unity. Müller overstates his point on this matter by suggesting that nationalism was Christian Democrat's 'prime ideological enemy'. Perhaps in the seventeenth century, during the rise of the nation state, the Roman Catholic Church regarded this force as a major ideological threat; but in the post-1945 era it had a variety of other, far more immediate, problems to worry about, such as communism, secularism, and selfish consumerism.

It is important to note that all mainstream political parties reacted to the catastrophes of the 1930s and the 1940s by adopting a similar outlook. The anti-nationalist sentiments adopted by Christian Democrats in the 1940s were motivated by a concern to avoid, or at least minimize, the disruptive impact of nationalist conflict on global security. However, the immediate post-war reaction to the politicization of nationalism was far more restricted in scope than today. In the twenty-first century it is not only political nationalism, but the very sense of national pride, that has been branded as problematic by those wedded to a federalist or cosmopolitan outlook.

Contemporary Christian Democrat's suspicion of nationalism is exemplified by the political orientation of the German CDU, particularly under the leadership of Angela Merkel. In recent years, but especially since the mass movement of migrants to Germany in 2015, Merkel has sought to draw a sharp contrast between her policies and those motivated by nationalist concerns. Müller claims that Merkel has, in effect, forced 'believers in Europe to choose between her own brand of "compassionate conservatism" and the "Christian national" vision of Fortress Europe, propounded by leaders such as Hungary's Viktor Orbán and Poland's Jaroslaw Kaczynski'.[19]

Müller is right to suggest that the difference separating Germany and Hungary on the migration question is not simply about the status of national borders: what is at stake are fundamental differences between the way that the sense of nationhood is understood. So when Orbán stated that EU member states 'should not be afraid of being good patriots', and added, the 'idea of nationalism is a danger for Europe is an idea I cannot accept', he implicitly drew attention to the sentiments that divide the two camps.[20] The term 'good patriot' no longer translates into a positive vision in the political vocabulary of the EU elites.

For the elites who are invested in European unification, nationalism represents the 'bad old days': but for a significant section of East European and Hungarian people, the sense of nationhood is still fundamental to their identity.

Hungary – a nationalism *sui generis*?

In recent decades, the conviction that national sentiments and attachments are responsible for all the woes that have afflicted modern European societies has acquired the status of a taken-for-granted truth within international cultural and political institutions. In particular, the EU promotes a political narrative that depicts nationalism as itself the cause of war and political violence. The conservative British philosopher Roger Scruton refers to the 'founding myth' of European integration, the claim that 'belief that nationhood and national self-determination were the prime causes of the wars that had ruined Europe'.[21]

Promoters of the EU continually justify the existence of their institutions on the grounds that they have successfully prevented the outbreak of yet another nationalism-driven European war. At the same time, they caution against complacency and call for vigilance against the possible resurgence of such conflicts. Warning of the 'demons of nationalism' Jean-Claude Juncker, the former prime minister of Luxembourg and head of the EU Commission, pointed to the growth of nationalist parties in Europe and stated that 'I am chilled by the realization of how similar circumstances in Europe in 2013 are to those of 100 years ago'.[22]

Although in theory, EU policymakers are prepared to make a distinction between patriotism and nationalism, in practice they tend to view all forms of national sentiment with suspicion. They are particularly suspicious of expressions of national sentiment in the Eastern part of the continent, which even today is sometimes described as a form of 'Balkan tribalism'. As one EU official warned during the Yugoslav conflict, 'if we do not Brusselize them, they will Balkanize us'.[23] A similar sentiment informs the animosity directed by advocates of European federalism towards Hungary. They frequently attack this nation's celebration of national symbols and sentiments for its violation of their post-modern and post-national ethos and denounce the importance that the Hungarian government attaches to the promotion of national identity as an affront to the anti-national and multicultural philosophy of the EU. Consequently, Hungarian nationalism is often depicted as a unique and particularly virulent strand of xenophobia.

The language used to castigate the Hungarian sense of nationhood often adopts a strident and emotional tone. Hungarian nationalism is often depicted as a unique and a particularly toxic variant of this ideology. This sentiment was forcefully expressed by Bono, of the rock band U2, when he informed an American Senate subcommittee that the reaction by 'hyper-nationalist' Hungary and Poland to the migration crisis represented an 'existential threat' to Europe.[24] The use of the term 'existential threat' was self-consciously used to raise the temperature and signal the warning that unless something was done, it was only a matter of time before the jackboots were back on the streets of Budapest.

Commentators frequently assert that Hungarian political culture lacks any genuine democratic traditions and is therefore exceptionally authoritarian or chauvinist. Writing in this vein, a commentator for *Al Jazeera* claimed that:

> The Hungarians obviously never embraced the culture of democracy, opting instead for a powerful authoritarian leader who shifts blame to everyone else but them for the miserable state of the country. Orbán's tirades against the EU, the West and Hungary's other perceived enemies obviously find resonance in the country.[25]

Other commentaries focus on the supposed insecurity of Hungarian national identity and its defensive, even pathological, dimensions. One commentator writes that 'there is hardly another country that swings as radically between the emotional extremes of nationalist megalomania and deep-seated feelings of guilt'.[26] From this perspective, the allegedly toxic nationalist culture of contemporary Hungary is depicted as merely the most recent variant of the nation's age-old legacy. As one exposition of the defects of Hungarian exceptionalism insists:

> When observing the ugly manifestations of extremism in Hungary or the maverick policies of its current government, foreign commentators usually perceive the underlying nationalist sentiments, but tend to interpret them as just another brand of nationalism in 'New Europe'. Hungarian nationalism, however, stands out in central Europe. It is particularly forceful and, to use a mild term, nervous. It is always on the alert, wary of possible vicious attacks and lashing out when no one would expect, as there was no apparent or unprovoked offence.[27]

According to the stereotype of a 'particularly forceful' Hungarian nationalism, this is an irrational, highly volatile, and *sui generis* phenomenon.

The claim that Hungarian nationalism is in a class of its own is a contention that echoes criticisms directed at Hungary's political culture since the nineteenth century. It emerged during the debates that surrounded the nationalities question in the Habsburg Empire in the late nineteenth and early twentieth centuries.[28] That similar criticisms continue to be re-raised in the very different context of the twenty-first century serves as testimony to the durability of historical stereotypes and the prejudices they invoke.

It is frequently argued that nationalism in Hungary has always been different and far more unstable than those of other European societies. Writing of the apparent resurgence of a 'Hungarian ethnic nationalism' which 'deploys increasingly irredentist themes', a commentary in the *National Interest* in 2015 warned that 'Hungary as a source of countervailing trends with Europe should come as no surprise' since 'Hungary has always been a land of contradictions'.[29]

The historian Peter Sugar, in his essay 'The More It Changes, the More Hungarian Nationalism Remains the Same', forcefully advances the assertion that Hungarian nationalism has always contained an inherent aggressive and xenophobic dimension. He notes that:

> The literature dealing with Magyar nationalism is extensive. The general impression created by its manifestations during the last roughly two and a half centuries has been that it had been aggressive and disrespectful of the rights of other nations living in the lands of historical Hungary, occasionally even bordering on the criminal. This evaluation did not originate with R. W. Seton-Watson . . . [British historian] . . . but was certainly disseminated widely by the works he published under the pen names of Viator and Scotus Viator. While some of the judgments passed on Magyar nationalism were exaggerated and even unjustified, the correctness of the general picture cannot be denied.[30]

That Hungarian nationalism has had its dark side is not in doubt. But the claim that this nationalism was always driven by destructive passions and possessed no positive qualities overlooks the changing contours of its history. For example, the Hungarian Revolution of 1848 was widely and rightly interpreted as an enlightened attempt to achieve freedoms usually associated with the nineteenth-century version of liberal democracy. The pathologization of Hungarian nationalism also ignores and minimizes the destructive and distortive influence of wider regional and global conflicts on Hungarian society through the centuries.

At times, Hungarian nationalist politicians behaved oppressively towards ethnic minorities within the Habsburg Empire. But as the historian Stephen Borsody explains, the oppression of minorities by Magyar elites in the decades leading up to the Great War was far from unique to Hungary:

> Neither assimilation motivated by the ideal of the homogeneous nation state, nor alliances to serve nationalist interests, are uniquely Hungarian phenomena. Hungary's neighbours had committed similar, and sometimes even worse, crimes in the pursuit of nationalist objectives, in particular after the Second World War.[31]

Nevertheless, propaganda during the First World War ensured that Hungarian nationalism gained a reputation as a particularly evil political force. The portrait drawn by Eduard Benes, the Czech nationalist leader, of the corrosive impact of the Magyars on regional stability resonated with the outlook of some policymakers in France and Britain during the First World War. In his essay 'Detruisez l'Autriche-Hongrie!', Benes held the Magyars responsible for the outbreak of the 1914 War, blaming Hungarians for the promotion of the Habsburg Empire's anti-Slav Balkan policy, which in turn was depicted as the trigger for the conflict that led to the outbreak of the First World War.[32]

If there is an element of continuity that appears to transcend historical time, it is the way that Magyar nationalism has been represented and subjected to a double standard of moral evaluation. The contribution of the British historian Robert William Seton-Watson is paradigmatic in this respect. Seton-Watson's book *Racial Problems in Hungary*, published in 1908, had huge impact on the way that Hungary came to be regarded in Great Britain and large parts of the Western world. At the time Seton-Watson was regarded as the leading international expert on Hungary. During the First World War, he became an advisor to the British Foreign Office; and following the war, he and some of his like-minded colleagues played an important role in influencing the proceedings of the Paris Peace Conference. One fateful outcome of these proceedings was the enactment of the Treaty of Trianon in June 1920.

The Treaty of Trianon is widely perceived by Hungarians as one of the greatest tragedies that befell this nation in modern times. The treaty led to the dismemberment of Hungary, leaving three million Hungarians (one-third of ethnic Hungarians) outside the borders of this newly-constructed geographical entity. From the standpoint of Seton-Watson's critique of Hungarian nationalism, the punishment inflicted on this country was a proportionate price to pay for the previous inequities perpetuated by Magyar nationalists on other ethnic groups in the Austro-Hungarian Empire.

In his Preface to *Racial Problems In Hungary*, Seton-Watson argued that, unlike other students of the Dual Monarchy, he gradually came to the conclusion that the 'racial question in Austria is far less difficult and less important than the racial question in Hungary'.[33] In other words, he concluded that the cause of the problem of nationalities and ethnic tension that afflicted the Habsburg Empire lay not in Vienna but in Budapest, and Magyar chauvinism was singled out as a malevolent force that was far more selfish and destructive than the other nationalist movements in the Austro-Hungarian Empire.

There is no doubt that the Hungarian authorities were, at times, callous and brutal towards ethnic minorities. Their coercive Magyarisation policies directed at other ethnic groups were unjust and inevitably provoked hostility and resentment. However Seton-Watson's presentation of this problem one-sidedly relieves all other parties of moral responsibility for the nationality problems that plagued the Hapsburg Empire. What is also striking about this study of *Racial Problems* is the author's singular lack of self-consciousness about his own 'racial problems' with Hungarians and Jews.

The way in which Seton-Watson adopted the racial outlook and rhetoric of his times is not unusual in early twentieth century historiography. It is important to adopt a balanced view of the turn of the twentieth-century discussion on the nationalities in question and not to judge the protagonists in accordance with the conventions and standards of the contemporary era. However, what strikes the twenty-first-century reader is the casual manner with which this critic of 'racial problems' embraces dubious racial stereotypes. Re-reading *Racial Problems* and some of Seton-Watson's other works, it is difficult to know whether the real culprits in his story were the Hungarian political elites or the Jews who so enthusiastically and dramatically assimilated into Magyar society. Time and again, he accused the Magyar elites of allowing their society to come under Jewish domination, writing of the 'all powerful Jewish publican and usurer' who used their influence to control the outcome of local elections' at the expense of the non-Magyar nationalities.[34]

Seton-Watson pointed out that during the nineteenth century, Hungary's relatively liberal attitude towards Jewish people encouraged the latter to wholeheartedly embrace a Magyar nationalist identity. He seems to believe that it was not sincere conviction but opportunism that led Jewish people to embrace Magyar culture. Seton-Watson expressed dismay at this development, since he believed that Jewish support for the Magyarisation of the region assisted the project of oppressing ethnic minorities in Hungary: remarking that 'the Catholic Church and the Jews form today the two chief bulwarks of Magyar chauvinism'. Seton-Watson also condemned Jews for using the freedom they were granted to assume a dominant position over Hungarian culture and the economy. In his discussion of the local government reforms of 1886, he remarked that 'its true significance lay in its unnamed but no less real concessions to the growing Jewish bourgeoisie, who cunningly assumed a mask of Magyar Chauvinism, in order to gain control of the finance, the trade and the municipal government of the country'. He criticized the Magyar magnates and gentry for being 'blinded by racial ardour' and accepting Jews as 'valuable allies in the national struggle', adding that 'too late they have awakened' to the 'fact that not only the towns, to which they were indifferent, but even the counties are falling more and more to Jewish hands';[35] and lamented the fact that 'in the twentieth century trade, finance and journalism have well-nigh become a Jewish monopoly in Hungary'.[36]

Although at the time, Seton-Watson's distaste towards Jewish culture was shared by many Anglo-American intellectuals, his tendency to regard turn of the century Hungary as a veritable Jewish fiefdom struck some of his correspondents as unworthy of a serious scholar. The Hungarian liberal social scientist Oszkár Jászi regarded Seton-Watson's writings favourably and corresponded regularly with him. But even he was taken aback by Seton-Watson's casual anti-Semitic reference to the domination of Hungary by the Jews. In his 1911 study *The Southern Slav Question and the Habsburg Monarchy*, Seton-Watson noted that 'in Hungary the Jews alone are triumphant in politics, in the Press, in finance, in commerce'; and he warned that the Austrian anti-Semitic politician, Karl Lueger's 'offensive gibes at the "Judaeo-Magyars" contain a painful element of truth; for Hungary is in danger of becoming a Zionist rather than a Magyar national state'.[37] In his review of *The Southern Slav Question*, Jászi could not let this remark pass and noted that 'our distinguished English colleague allowed himself to be influenced by the worst kind of Christian Socialist petty bourgeois ideology'.[38]

Jászi was of course aware of the pernicious role of Lueger in the public affairs of the Habsburg Empire. Lueger, the mayor of Vienna and leader of the anti-Semitic Christian Socialist Party, was bitterly hostile to Hungarians, and his animosity towards them was only exceeded by his detestation of Jewish people. He coined the term 'Judeo-Magyar' to express his hatred for both Jews and Hungarians.[39] His identification of Magyars and Jews as the twin evils afflicting the Habsburg Empire expressed attitudes that, in a more restrained form, were similar to those of Seton-Watson.

However one assesses the scholarly value of Seton-Watson's work, it is difficult to avoid the conclusion that he did not hold himself to the rigorous standard of non-racial probity that he applied to Hungarian society. His own uncritical use of racial categories to interpret historical development indicates that his version of *Racial Problems in Hungary* were not untainted by the faults that he attributed to the targets of his polemic.

One of Seton-Watson's British collaborators was Henry Wickham Steed, the correspondent of the *Times* in Vienna. During the First World War, both men were appointed co-directors of propaganda directed against Austria-Hungary and played an important role providing advice to Western negotiators involved in drawing up the post-war peace treaty. Steed, like Seton-Watson, had previously drawn the conclusion that Hungarians were a destabilizing influence on the region and the cause of most of the problems of the Austrian-Hungarian Empire. And like Seton-Watson, he discerned the influence of shadowy Jewish interests behind developments in Austria-Hungary.

Henry Wickham Steed's book *The Habsburg Monarchy*, published in 1913, is interesting for its portrayal of Magyar nationalism as the helpless victim of a Jewish conspiracy. He wrote that 'in truth, there is no Hungarian question' – there is a 'Jewish question, and this terrible race means not only to master one of the great warrior nations in the world, but it means, and is consciously striving, to enter the lists against the other great race of the north (the Russians)'.[40] Echoing Seton-Watson's concern about 'Judaeo-Magyars', Steed reminded his readers that Budapest is 'commonly nick-named "Judapest"'.[41]

The role of the critics of Judaeo-Magyar nationalism in contributing to the subsequent emergence of the thesis of a Hungarian nationalism *sui generis* remains a subject that is rarely explored in the historical and sociological literature. Yet it was a term that was sufficiently influential to enter the vocabulary of some policymakers and diplomats in the interwar era. For example, the historian Gusztáv Kecskés cites the French Consul in Kolozsvár (Cluj-Napoca), writing in 1928 about the Judaeo-Magyars – that is, Jews who identified with Magyar aspirations in Transylvania.[42]

It is worth noting in passing that critics who fiercely criticize Hungarian anti-Semitic nationalist politics of the interwar period tend to give a free pass to the anti-Semitic sentiments directed against Hungarian Judaeo-Magyar nationalism. This selective approach towards assessing the character of Hungarian nationalism continues to this day.

During the post-First World War peace negotiations, the views expressed by Steed and Seton-Watson about Hungarian political culture clearly influenced the attitudes of the British Foreign Office negotiators. One Foreign Office official, Harold Nicolson, made no attempt to hide his anti-Hungarian prejudices. In his recollection of the proceedings of the peace conference Nicolson wrote:

> My feelings toward Hungary were less detached. I confess that I regarded, and still regard, that Turanian tribe with acute distaste. Like their cousins the Turks, they had destroyed much and created nothing. Buda Pest was a false city devoid of any autochthonous reality. For centuries the Magyars had oppressed their subject nationalities. The hour of liberation and retribution was at hand.[43]

Nicolson's 'distaste' directed at Hungarians and their 'false city' communicated a spirit of chauvinism that implied that Magyar society and culture were devoid of any redeeming features.

The exotic othering of the Turanian tribe – allegedly the ancestors of the Finno-Ugric people like the Magyars – has continued to influence Western perceptions of Hungarian society. As late as the early 1980s, an essay published in *National Geographic* informed its readers that, 'by all rights, some say, the Hungarians should not be in Hungary at all; if their language is incomprehensible to their neighbors, if their history has been problematic, it is their own doing'. The author poses the question of 'where have they come from' and speculates that probably 'just East of the Urals in Western Siberia'.[44] The sentiment that this tribe of exotic non-Western people are not like their geographical neighbours is rarely expressed in explicit terms in the twenty-first century. However such views served to legitimate the post-First World War settlement, which had such destructive consequences for Hungarian society.

The Treaty of Trianon fundamentally altered the inner content of Hungarian national identity and weakened its civic dimension. Contrary to some of the Orientalist literature that presents Hungarian nationalism as essentially ethnic or tribalist, at times it's far more civic than some of its Western counterparts. As Robert Bideleux notes, the nationalism of the kingdom of Hungary was 'more "civil" and "cosmopolitan" than "ethnic", while those that developed in some of Europe's "western fringes" (Ireland, Scotland, the Basque country, Catalonia) as well as Belgium, Scandinavia and Germany were decidedly ethnic'.[45] The dismemberment of Hungary led to the fragmentation and separation of different Magyar communities. No longer bound together by an affiliation to the institution of a common Hungarian nation state, there occurred a distinct shift from a civic to a cultural form of national identity.

The thesis of the continuity of Hungarian nationalism fails to grasp the importance of this dramatic moment and the shift in the form of national identity that occurred in the post-Trianon era. During the interwar era, the civic conception of nationhood that prevailed in the late nineteenth and early twentieth century gradually gave way to an emphasis on the cultural practices and attitudes that bound together otherwise geographically dispersed Hungarian communities.

Hungarian nationalist sentiment could never reconcile itself to the legacy of Trianon. During the interwar era, the sentiment of resentment and vengeance fostered a climate where nationalism acquired a self-destructive and racial dimension. The fantasy that under German hegemony Hungary could regain its lost territory and its people could be reunited encouraged groups of nationalists to support the Nazi cause. However after the Second World, under Soviet occupation, it became evident to most Hungarians that the geographical reality of the post-Trianon era was unlikely to be reversed.

During the period of Soviet occupation, Hungarian society was under powerful pressure to break from its historical past, to the point that there was little outlet for expressing national sentiments or for the cultivation of a Hungarian identity. Following the Stalinist takeover of Hungary in 1948, the very idea of the nation was denounced as an outdated and reactionary institution. The Soviet-imposed puppet regimes actively discouraged Hungarians from publicly discussing the fate of their brethren in the surrounding regions. As the Hungarian philosopher János Kis noted, 'until about the end of the 1960s, the mere fact of the existence of ethnic Hungarians beyond the borders of Hungary was largely ignored within the country'.[46] Borsody noted that as a result 'despite the seriousness of the problem, the world seldom hears of the Hungarian minorities', pointing out that an 'official silence' was 'imposed on Hungary, a member-state of the Soviet bloc, as a fraternal obligation to Communist solidarity'.[47]

The quarantine that the Soviet-dominated regimes imposed on the manifestation of Hungarian national identity meant that Trianon and its legacy could not be discussed and debated in public. As one study published in 1983 noted, 'during the past three-and-a-half decades the open discussion or teaching of the nature and impact of this . . . [Trianon] . . . treaty has been a taboo in Hungary.[48] The policing of the memory of Trianon by the communist authorities was thoroughgoing. As an illustration of this trend, the historian Steven Vardy points out how a 'short and inoffensive article published by historian Karoly Vigh on the occasion of the sixtieth anniversary of Trianon' in 1980 was 'promptly withdrawn from circulation'.[49]

It was only towards the early 1980s that individual writers and intellectuals felt sufficiently confident to contest the taboo on Trianon. In 1981, the historian Peter Hanák published an essay in the literary periodical *Élet és Irodalom* that explored the consequences of this officially promoted amnesia. Hanák observed:

> We have been unable to digest Trianon consciously until our very own days. [After 1945] the whole complex problem of Trianon was placed on this list of those taboos that touched the path of nationalism. True, we did mention occasionally that the Treaty of Trianon was an unjust and an imperialistic peace. But we also added immediately that interwar revisionism was conceived in the nuptial bed of nationalism. Moreover, even though each of these assertions were true individually, and each contained valid value judgments, neither from a logical, nor from a psychological or consciousness point of view were we able to resolve the contradictions between them. This is all the more lamentable as without examining the lasting shock impact of Trianon, we can neither approach, nor hope to understand the Hungarian Weltanschauung and the Hungarian national consciousness in the twentieth century.[50]

The policing of Hungary's national memory profoundly influenced the significance that sections of this society attach to the cultivation of their national identity in the twenty-first century. It helps explain and place in perspective the renewed interest that sections of the Hungarian political establishment and the intelligentsia have in the forging of relationship between contemporary national identity and the historical symbols of the past.

Coming to terms with the past

In the post-Second World War era, it was not uncommon for societies to distance themselves from their historical past. The defeated Axis powers of Germany, Italy, and Japan were, in particular, under formidable pressure to acknowledge their war guilt and to avoid cultivating a national identity that was too closely linked to their past. Throughout the 1960 and 1970s, the legacy of the Nazi epoch made the attempts to revive a German identity an intensely sensitive issue. And yet the question could not be entirely ignored.

Franz Josef Strauss, one of Germany's leading post-war conservative politicians, argued in the course of the 1987 election campaign:

> It is high time that we emerge from the shadow of the Third Reich . . . and become a normal nation again . . . To idolise the nation is catastrophic and disastrous: but to deny the nation, to deny one's national identity, to destroy

our national identity, to refuse to return to it, to a purified national consciousness, is just as disastrous.[51]

Strauss' sentiments expressed views that were widely held by right-wing German
conservatives. But the importance of national sentiment and attachments was also
recognized by sections of German Social Democrats. In May 1981, following his
return from Israel, Social Democratic Chancellor Helmut Schmidt declared that
'German foreign policy can and will no longer be overshadowed by Auschwitz'.
His call to lift the burden of the legacy of the Holocaust on the direction of German foreign policy was reaffirmed by Christian Democrat Chancellor Helmut
Kohl in 1984.[52]

The *Historikerstreit* (1986–1987), the controversy that erupted between left- and
right-wing historians about how to interpret and remember Germany's Nazi past,
can also be seen as a debate about whether it was permissible to affirm and nor-
malize this nation's identity. Jürgen Habermas led the attack on the attempt by
conservative historians to reassert Germany's national traditions. However by this
time, even the leadership of the Social Democratic Party felt that the time had come
for Germany to come to remove the stigma of war memory. The intervention of
Social Democratic Party Secretary Peter Glotz during a debate on the role of the
past indicated that the quest to ground Germany's national identity in its history
had gained bipartisan support. Glotz stated;

> Is the search for one's own identity merely hocus-pocus? This is where I start
> to disagree with Jürgen Habermas. I doubt whether it is enough for democ-
> racy to base itself on a universalistic morality and a logical chain of reasoning,
> as for example in the text of our constitution. The need to take bearings and
> self-knowledge, but also self-confidence and pride from one's own history is
> not automatically right-wing.[53]

The debate on Germany's wartime past and its relevance for the country's future
indicated that the relationship between history and national identity could not be
simply evaded. As the German experience showed, the attempt to distance society
from its historical legacy and to discourage the cultivation of its national identity –
no matter how well-intentioned – tends to displace rather than solve the problem
it seeks to tackle.

The highly charged atmosphere surrounding the German history debate was
largely due to the formidable problems involved in the normalization of a past that
was so dramatically associated with the devastating experience of the Nazi era.
Whether or not it was acknowledged explicitly, the debate about how to come to
terms with the experience of the Holocaust served as a medium for attempting to
remove a significant obstacle to the reworking of a German national identity.

In the event, the German political and cultural elites opted for a course of action
that reframed national identity through the narrative of the *Good European*. Back in
December 1949, *Time Magazine* ran on its cover page the title 'Germany: A Good

European'. Thomas Mann's 1953 pronouncement that 'we do not want a German Europe, but a European Germany' expressed the dominant orientation of Germany's elites towards the construction of their nation's identity. As one study points out, 'the political elites of the Federal Republic of Germany have thoroughly Europeanized the German national identity since the 1950s'.[54]

This federalist consensus has remained remarkably stable up to the present time. Even after German reunification, this approach continued to define government policy, and, arguably, the emphasis on the European rather than national dimension reached its high point during Merkel's response to the migration crisis of 2015.

The Europeanization of German nation state identity was relatively successful and helped to create a situation where the tension between national sovereignty and federalist authority are comparatively easily managed. Moreover, in adopting the identity of the Good European, Germany has in effect demonstrated to the rest of the world that it had made the necessary amends for its past. In circumstances when German national interests are both realized and enforced through the EU, the argument that people's identity has become 'post-national' is at least plausible. Arguably that is why so many of the leading 'post-national' and cosmopolitan thinkers in Europe, including Jürgen Habermas and Ulrich Beck, are German. Their understandable revulsion towards Germany's past encourages their quest for a non-national and post-traditional identity.

Given the economic and political weight of Germany, it was possible for this country to realize its national aspirations by embracing the Europeanization of its identity. In practice the distinction that Thomas Mann drew between a European Germany and a German Europe had lost some of its relevance in the post-war epoch, as this country became the *de facto* economic hegemonic power in Europe. However, Germany's strategy of the Europeanization of its national identity was not an alternative that would work for some of the other EU member states.

For Eastern European societies, the Europeanization of national identity was not an option, but a condition of entry to the EU. In 2000, the EU's former Enlargement Commissioner Günter Verheugen laid down a doctrine 'which targeted the rise of populist and nationalist parties in Central and Eastern Europe before the accession'.[55] A study by Julian Pänke noted that this doctrine 'affirmed that a leading political role of any such parties in government after elections would block EU membership'. As Pänke explained:

> Before the parliamentary elections in Slovakia in 2002, Günter Verheugen reminded the electorate of the negative repercussions should they take the wrong choice. Thus, adherence to European norms supersedes the outcomes of free democratic elections.[56]

The terms on which East European states were allowed to join the EU clearly precluded them from promoting political sentiments that Verheugen had characterized as 'populist and nationalist'. Although sections of the East European elites, particularly members of the old *nomenklatura*, were enthusiastic about becoming 'European', significant sections of their society remained untouched by this sentiment.

From the German perspective, Günter Verheugen's strictures against East European states 'taking the wrong choice' made perfect sense. However from the perspective of recently freed states, such as Hungary, such external pressure on the exercise of national sovereignty represented a continuity with the kind of taboos that were previously imposed on the discussion of this country's national identity. Moreover, given the decades-long moratorium on public discussions on this subject, sentiments that had no opportunity to express themselves in the past would eventually find a way of gaining their voice.

After its accession to the EU, Hungary, along with some of the other East European states, was frequently lectured to follow the example of Germany and 'come to terms with its history'. The burden of its argument was to suggest that, having collaborated with the Nazis during the Second World War, Hungarians should follow the example of their German cousins and trade-in their nationalist past for a European future. What such commentaries overlook is that, unlike in Western European societies, the Hungarian historical imagination needed to process not only the experience of the Second World War but also the legacy of more than four decades of Soviet domination. Moreover, despite the unprecedented gravity of the Hungarian Holocaust for most Hungarians, the legacy of post-1948 totalitarianism has a far greater temporal immediacy.

In the Hungarian historical imagination, the sense of responsibility for the atrocities of the Second World War is mediated through the humiliating and oppressive experience of the Soviet-imposed puppet regimes that followed it. The Hungarian novelist Sándor Márai offers a compelling account of the workings of this dynamic in his *Memoir of Hungary 1944–1948*. Writing of the pillaging of the Hungarian countryside by Russian soldiers, he observed that, 'if there was some kind of guilty conscience because of the past in Hungarian society, the Russians' attitude and behaviour extinguished its last faint glimmer'.[57]

The divergent historical experience of East and Western societies has led to a differential orientation towards the national past. Having been forced to avoid discussions of important historical episodes, such as the Treaty of Trianon, Hungarians are understandably interested in recovering their national past. From the standpoint of a 'Europeanized' identity, the traditions of the past are irredeemably flawed: until the launching of the project of European unification, there were very few 'good old days' for the EU ideologue. In contrast, many people and political leaders in nations such as Hungary regard their historical traditions as the foundation on which their community is built. Hungarians might not have had many 'good old days', but many of them regard their historical experience as an important legacy for the generations of the future.

The denationalization of identity

By the time Hungary and other East European nations joined the EU, the terms on which questions to do with nationhood and national identity were discussed

had changed. During the *Historikerstreit* of the 1980s, the conservative right felt
sufficiently confident to reaffirm the national past. The essay by the German historian Ernst Nolte, titled 'The Past That Will Not Pass Away', which kicked off this
debate, exemplified a growing confidence in reasserting Germany's national tradition. However, within a few years, the terms on which the discussion of nationhood
was debated had acquired a defensive tone.

The *Historikerstreit* coincided with a moment where the advocates of European
federalism became increasingly wedded to the elaboration of a system of transnational values that explicitly sought to weaken national identities and sentiments
that were attached to the feeling of nationhood. This project was motivated by the
realization that in order to strengthen the legitimacy of the EU, people's cultural
attachment to their national affiliations needed to be weaker. The leaders of the EU
came to the conclusion that the success of the federalist project could not simply
rely on the maintenance of economic prosperity: people needed to identify with
European values. The concern that the European project was losing its appeal was
clearly articulated by the 1993 De Clercq report on the future public relations
strategy of the EU. This report was motivated by the recognition that 'for the first
time' there was 'a break in the traditional support of European citizens for the cause
of European integration', and added that 'for the first time, it would appear that
the worthiness of the "good project" – in other words, European construction and
integration – is being questioned'.[58]

Vincent Della Sala noted that the EU's foundational myth was based on the contrast drawn between itself and the destructive forces of nationalism in the 1930s and
1940s.[59] However, with the passage of time, simply reminding people of the memory of Nazism and of totalitarianism had become less and less effective in inspiring
loyalty to the EU project. As Chris Shore noted in his study *Building Europe: The
Cultural Politics of European Integration*, the EU sought to strengthen its legitimacy by
displacing people's national cultural perspective with a European one. This cultural
campaign attempted to promote a historical memory where Europe, rather than the
nation, enjoyed central status.

In the early 1990s, supporters of European federalism called for the 'Europeanization' of mass education and the rewriting of history. Shore reported that 'typically,
officials justify their attempts to promote the rewriting of history books to reflect
the "European perspective" on the grounds that this is necessary to combat the
hegemony of nationalist ideology, which they see as the principal obstacle to European Union'.[60] Pedro Correa Martín-Arroyo has described this project as one of
'histoeuropeanisation', by which he means the increasing historiographical conver-
gence witnessed in the last decades towards a 'more European' history of Europe,
'in detriment, to a certain extent, of the traditional national historical traditions'.[61]

As Martín-Arroyo explained, the principal objective of histoeuropeanisation was
to encourage denationalization of history:

> In recent years, an increasing number of politicians, intellectuals and insti-
> tutions have explicitly or implicitly expressed their wish to witness the

Europeanisation of the various national memories or even the emergence of a clearly distinct supranational European memory. In fact, some countries have been urged to harmonise their memory laws according to a certain European standard. As a consequence, the interpretation of the past is becoming less and less a 'national privilege'. It could be said indeed that we are witnessing the process of the 'denationalisation of history', by which the 'competences' of history and memory are being reallocated from the national to the European supranational sphere.[62]

This quest to denationalize history also coincided with a more thoroughgoing strategy of discrediting the national feeling of belonging.

During the 1990s, cosmopolitanism emerged as a central element of the European federalist self-consciousness. Cosmopolitan theory emphasized the inferiority of the national to the transnational consciousness. It also celebrated cultural diversity as a fundamental value that represented an enlightened alternative to an outdated and allegedly monolithic national identity. In effect, diversity became 'celebrated constantly as a core European value'.[63] Initially the concept of diversity was used by the EU elites to refer to the 'diversity of national cultures'. However by the turn of the twenty-first century, it was employed not to defend national cultures but to devalue them. Increasingly, national cultures were represented as artificial entities designed to negate the heterogeneity of real life. From this perspective, national consciousness represented a threat to the diverse minorities that inhabited a common geographical space. Squeezed between a transnational cosmopolitanism and diverse minority identities, there was simply no legitimate place for national cultures.

The de-legitimation of nationalism along with the celebration of cultural diversity gained significant influence amongst European academics, cultural entrepreneurs, and policymakers. One influential advocate of this outlook was Ulrich Beck. Beck's attachment to a transnational *Weltanschauung* was motivated by the conviction that politics had to be 'deterritorialised' and identities 'denationalised'. His call to 'denationalize' national politics was justified in part on the grounds that national politics had become ineffective in a globalized world. But his more fundamental objection to the nation state was that, through its exclusionary powers, it violated the new sacred principle of diversity. That is why he supported 'overcoming the lie of the national age that says: basic rights can be divided by nation – and denied to everybody else'.[64]

Beck claimed that 'nation states embody the denial of diversity' and asserted that states 'represent a threat to their own domestic diversity, to the multiple loyalties associated with the flows and exchanges that take place within their borders'.[65] For Beck and his fellow cosmopolitans, diversity assumed a status that verged on the sacred. An article he co-wrote with the leading British sociologist Anthony Giddens stated that 'from a cosmopolitan point of view, diversity is not the problem; it is the solution'.[66] The question – solution to what? – was answered by the title of the article: 'Nationalism has become the enemy of Europe's nations'.

At first sight the transformation of a physical fact – diversity – into a moral value makes little sense. Diversity is not used simply as a synonym for a plural or multi-ethnic society. It is not only a term of description but a quasi-moral category that attributes superiority of heterogeneity over homogeneity. Promoters of diversity often display a sense of loathing towards homogenous social arrangements, especially ones that are rooted in community tradition. Habermas regards concepts like 'the people' or 'the nation' as a dangerous fantasy used by 'right wing populism' to undermine diversity. He explains his antipathy to national consciousness in the following terms:

> After half a century of labour immigration, even the European peoples, given their ethnic, linguistic and religious diversity, can no longer be conceived as culturally homogeneous entities.[67]

Müller echoes Habermas' disdain for the people and asserts that 'the idea of the single, homogeneous, authentic people is a fantasy'.[68]

In fact, the fantasy is the belief that homogeneity is an essential ingredient of national consciousness or of movements that are characterized as populist. Homogeneity plays a role in racial nationalism, such as National Socialism. But to make a conceptual leap from the Nazi focus on racial purity to claim that all forms of nationalism and populism are devoted to a homogeneous ideal of nation is an exercise in polemical acrobatics rather than serious analysis.

The purpose of transforming diversity into a value is that it can be operationalized to corrode and undermine national and indeed community attachments. The ideological politicization of diversity is oriented towards the project of undermining majority cultures within a nation and related appeals to 'the people'. To realize this ambition, concepts like 'the people' or 'the nation' are not simply depicted as illegitimate – they are also treated as fantasies and illusions that are the product of the imagination of malevolent populists. In this vein, Müller dismisses any claim to speak for or represent the people as a 'metapolitical illusion':

> The term *illusion* is justified here. For the whole people can never be grasped and represented – not least because it never remains the same, not even for a minute: citizens die, new citizens are born. Yet it is always tempting to claim that one can actually know the people as such.[69]

That people change is, like birth and death, a fact of life. But the attempt to convert a biological fact into a political argument against the endeavour to represent the people exposes the absence of substantive content of diversity.

Historical claims to represent the people may have, at times, been self-serving or misplaced, but they have not been founded on the assertion of actually speaking for every individual. What is 'grasped and represented' are not biological entities but the sentiments, interests, traditions, and practices through which a people are constituted. Speaking for the people in its different political forms has always been central to the principle of democratic representation.

Paradoxically, the valuation of diversity works as the mirror-image of the eighteenth- and nineteenth-century worship of pure homogenous communities. It is also redolent of a double standard. While national identities are deplored for treating their citizens as if they were homogenous, the diverse identities that trump the appeal to 'the people' are held to a different standard,[70] with minorities and identity groups invariably represented as if they all speak with one voice. The flip-side of diversity in Western society has been the fossilization of minority group identity and the homogenization of social and cultural experience, which is far more dominant amongst anti-populists than their opponents. The language of identity politics is replete with rigid and grotesquely essentialized assumptions. From this standpoint, the cultural identity conferred by race, ethnicity, gender, sexuality, or lifestyle choice defines the individual members of the group.

One inconsistency of the representation of diversity as an unquestionable value is that, in its application, it encourages a relativist indifference towards the values of minorities. Diversity in theory has meant multiculturalism in practice. Many multiculturalists, who insist that national identity is an artificial construction, take a very different approach to 'multi' identities. Multiculturalism relentlessly promotes the idea of acceptance and discourages the questioning of people's beliefs and lifestyles. Its dominant value is non-judgmentalism – but with one important caveat: it is prepared to decry national identity as exclusionary while treating other identities as inclusive.

Anti-nationalist supporters of diversity and cosmopolitanism often support what they call *constitutional patriotism* as an alternative to loyalty to the nation state. This concept, which emerged in post-war West Germany, proposed a form of legalistic patriotism that focused on procedures and rights rather than historical identities.[71] For Müller, the main advantage of constitutional patriotism is that it helps provide a medium for those who are looking for a 'post-national' or non-traditional attachment for 'increasingly multicultural societies'.[72] The chief target of promoters of constitutional patriotism is the sense of traditional – homogenous – nationhood.

The target of constitutional patriots is not simply extreme nationalism, nor even only conservative or right-wing nationalism. Not even civic nationalism escapes responsibility for encouraging homogeneity and marginalizing diversity. Müller contends that civic nationalism 'still aims at homogeneity among citizens'. He also objects to liberal nationalism on the ground that it:

> essentially reifies 'national culture' and is likely to opt for immigration and integration policies that are highly assimilationist; it's also more likely to place limits on political dissent and insist, for instance, that heroic national histories can't be questioned since they allegedly need to serve as sources of "national pride".[73]

In other words, it is the *national* quality of a culture that is the object of this critique. From this standpoint, the apotheosis of diversity makes perfect sense. The positive qualities attached to diversity, heterogeneity, multiculturalism, and anti-assimilationism are that they divest the state of any cultural and national underpinning. The nation state becomes denuded of cultural content.

The stigmatization of assimilation is an important message communicated through the anti-populist cultural script. From this perspective, the American tradition of assimilation, as expressed through the metaphor of the melting pot, is treated with scorn. The very principle of attempting to assimilate people from diverse backgrounds into a common community is often portrayed as unjust and exclusionary. The condemnation of assimilation is, as Müller indicates, inspired by a disdain for the valuation of a national community. The anti-assimilationist orientation towards upholding cultural segmentation and multiculturalism exposes the hollow content of its narrative of cosmopolitanism.

The imperative that animates the advocacy of constitutional patriotism is the desire to decouple 'the majority culture from the wider political culture'.[74] Through substituting loyalty to rules and procedures, cultural and national traditions cease to have a significant role in political life. In effect, a system based on loyalty to rules and procedures would be detached from any sense of historical continuity, sense of nationhood, or even pre-political loyalties to community traditions. One account explained the outcomes of this decoupling process in the following terms:

> In as far as this process of decoupling is successful, it breaks the historical link between republicanism and nationalism and shifts the solidarity of citizens onto a constitutional patriotism, which re-directs citizens' sense of loyalty and attachment away from pre-political entities such as the nation, ethnos or the family and towards the fundamental principles enshrined in the political culture and the basic law . . .
>
> Membership of the nation of citizens no longer rests upon an appeal to a shared language or common ethical and cultural origins, but merely reflects a shared political culture based upon standard liberal constitutional principles.[75]

For constitutional patriots like Habermas, even a shared language serves as an obstacle to the detachment of people from their historical and cultural traditions. That is why a transnational institution based on technical regulatory instruments and process like the EU is perceived as the terrain where the denationalization of political identity could flourish.

Experience has shown that the politicization of diversity, and attempts to decouple majority culture from political life, rarely lead to the flourishing of constitutional patriotism. Loyalty to process does not provide a foundation for political unity. Perversely, the main accomplishment of the cosmopolitan advocacy of diversity has not been the separation of culture and politics. While it has helped to undermine the status and authority of majority culture, arguably the institutionalization of diversity, paralleled by the proliferation of process, has led to the growth of the politics of identity. It is a testimony to the narrow technical vision of contemporary cosmopolitanism that its worship of heterogeneity has contributed to the current cultural valuation of parochial identity politics: hardly a Kantian vision of a universalist world citizen.

Historically the encouragement of the non-national and narrow particularism of diversity politics was associated with imperial ambitions. Empires as different as the Roman, Ottoman, British, and Habsburg empires encouraged the decoupling of culture and politics in an attempt to enforce their imperial domination. In the case of the British Empire, the politicization of diversity was pursued through the policy of Indirect Rule. One of the unhappy consequences of this policy was the cultivation of tribal identity. The divisive consequence of tribalism in Africa is a destructive legacy that haunts the continent to this day.

Not surprisingly, the politicization of diversity by twenty-first-century cosmopolitanism has close affinity with the idea of denationalizing identity in an imperial context. In their study *Cosmopolitan Europe*, Ulrich Beck and co-author Edgar Grande proposed using 'the concept of *empire* to describe the novel forms of political authority which are acquiring exemplary shape in Europe'.[76] Beck and Grande idealize the EU as a 'cosmopolitan empire' or a post-imperial empire based not on 'national demarcation and conquest, but on overcoming national borders, voluntarism, consensus, transnational interdependence and the political added value accruing from cooperation'.[77] For Beck and Grande, 'overcoming national borders' through the construction of a cosmopolitan empire is the natural progression from the messy world of demarcated nations.

The close connection between cosmopolitan theorists and the EU is grounded in their common mistrust of, and aversion to, the nation state. As Beck explained, 'the concept of the cosmopolitan state is based on the principle of national indifference towards the state.' Using a historical analogy with the separation of religion and state that was ratified by the Treaty of Westphalia in 1648, Beck contends that global stability would now be enhanced by the '*separation of state from nation*'.[78]

On paper, a cosmopolitan empire run by a world government can appear as an attractive alternative to the messy business of national politics. However, nations and the borders that divide them are not simply the redundant relic of history. They provide the historical foundation and geographical space on which popular sovereignty can be exercised. As the Hungarian social theorist István Bibo explained, 'the nation seems to be the largest political community with which the majority today are able to communicate without difficulty'. He argued:

> Beyond the limits of the nation people feel foreign. The framework of the nations and its state provide the conditions for successful communal activity, within the comprehension of people. This is so regardless of size: it applies to small and great, and even to irrationally formed national communities, and is independent of any ideology. This is the state of affairs today between the nation and the nation state on the one hand and higher forms of integration on the other.[79]

Bibo's comments were not directed at attempts to forge transnational institutions but against the denial of the centrality of the nation state for the pursuit of 'successful communal activity'.

During his presidency of the EC, Barroso spoke enthusiastically of the EU's transformation into an empire. 'We are a very special construction unique in the history of mankind,' stated Barroso in July 2007. He noted that 'sometimes I like to compare the EU as a creation to the organisation of empire', and added 'what we have is the first non-imperial empire'.[80] In reality, the EU is far from being an empire. That it has imperial ambitions is not in doubt. That it welcomes any expression of the denationalization of political identity is absolutely clear. But despite its best efforts, it has not succeeded in displacing historical national attachment with loyalty to its transnational institutions.

Constitutional patriots are intuitively attracted to the imperial ideal. From their perspective nationalist movements in Europe not only represent the antithesis of their preferred denationalized political identity; they also threaten the integrity of the Empire. Some of Hungary's fiercest Western intellectual critics sublimate their cosmopolitan disdain for this society through calls on the EU to intervene and punish its nationalist minded government. For example, Jan-Werner Müller has written at length about the need to safeguard democracy in the EU by countering 'recent illiberal turns in Hungary and Romania' through intervention. His 'principled' – in effect, imperial – argument for intervention in Hungarian domestic politics is justified on the grounds that what happens in this society has immediate consequences for all citizens of member states:

> Every European citizen has an interest in not being faced with an illiberal member state in the EU. After all, that state will make decisions in the European Council and therefore, at least in an indirect way, govern the lives of all citizens. Strictly speaking, there are no purely internal affairs in EU member states; all EU citizens are affected by developments in a particular member state. It might be true that there are far-away countries containing people about whom we know nothing – but as long as they are in the EU, they concern us.[81]

It is paradoxical that an argument that begins with a call to protect 'liberal democracy' in the EU member states from the illiberal turn of Hungary and Romania concludes with a very illiberal call for imperial intervention. This example shows that the spirit of constitutional patriotism is not motivated by the virtues of democracy, but a disdain for nationhood.

In one sense it is understandable that Hungary has become the object of cosmopolitan resentment. More than most European societies, Hungary has remained relatively immune to calls for celebrating diversity and multiculturalism. Since the regime change in the late 1980s, political leaders recognized that they could not remain indifferent to the goal of cultivating a Hungarian national identity. József Antall, the first prime minister of post-transition Hungary, who represented the Hungarian Democratic Forum, argued that 'we are convinced that the idea of the

nation has not lost its relevance by the end of the twentieth century'.[82] The durability of such sentiments is in part a reaction to previous attempts to prevent the
Hungarian public from openly engaging with its national identity.

Advocates of diversity continually declare that homogeneous communities are a
fiction and that twenty-first-century people live in multi-ethnic and diverse societies. From this perspective, Hungary is a diversity ideologue's nightmare. Even bitter
critics of Hungarian nationalism are forced to recognize that 'in reality Hungary
remains an overwhelmingly homogeneous population'.[83] That is why, even if Hungary had the most 'enlightened' government in the world, wedded to every value
invented by the Brussels bureaucracy, it would still stand accused of not taking the
promotion of diversity seriously.

Concluding remarks

No sooner did Barroso declare his enthusiasm for the 'first non-imperial empire'
than the conflict between rival national interests surfaced within the EU. From this
point onwards, the war of words directed at manifestations of national consciousness
acquired a new intensity.

During the Eurozone crisis of 2009–2010, the concern that people would be looking for national solutions to the economic crisis lead - consistency, lead to an escalation
of the anti-nationalist rhetoric of EU leaders. According to one study of this reaction:

> These were far more than exaggerated attempts at fear mongering by those
> frustrated with public opinion which seemed to be reverting back to national
> narratives. They were evocations of one of the most enduring political beliefs
> of the European Union: that only an integrated Europe stood between
> stability and peace, on the one hand, and a return to the nightmare of twentieth-
> century instability and war fuelled by ideology, particularly nationalism, on
> the other. European leaders sought to transform a complex economic and
> governance crisis into simple, understandable terms which provided reasons
> why governing should take place at the European level. It was the past, sym-
> bolized by war and nationalism, which gave reason for the present and the
> future status quo of European integration.[84]

It was in this context that the anti-national ethos of European federalism became
increasingly explicit, leading to the emergence of a narrative that treats virtually any
form of nationalism as the xenophobic foe of diversity.

As we will discuss in the next chapter, the focus on the denationalization of
identity was fixed, not only on the present, but also on the past. The denationalization of memory is also one of the by-products of the propaganda war directed at
national sovereignty. Writing of twenty-first century Germany, the historian Christian Meier remarks that 'national identity has ceased to be of great moment'. For
Meier, this development is closely linked to 'the extent to which historical consciousness has diminished in political associations within the country'.[85] Differences

in attitude towards national consciousness and identity are intimately linked to the conflict between the German/EU vision of the relationship of the present to the past, and that held by Hungary.

Notes

1 *Nationalism as a Religion* (1926) is available online – www.panarchy.org/hayes/nationalism. html.
2 Hayes (1926) p. 278.
3 Hobson (1988) p. 4.
4 Kohn (1946) p. 543.
5 Kohn (1946) p. 543.
6 See Count Carlo Sforza (1943) p. 113.
7 Herz (1951) (originally published in 1944).
8 Herz (1951) p. 1.
9 Deutsch (1969) p. 3.
10 Möhring & Prins (2013) p. 1.
11 Cited in Jaume (2010) p. 157.
12 Bendix (1978) p. 596.
13 See interview with Beck in *SightandSound*; 20 November 2007, www.signandsight.com/features/1603.html.
14 Churchill's speech is available at www.historiasiglo20.org/europe/anteceden2.htm.
15 www.historiasiglo20.org/europe/anteceden2.htm.
16 Risso (2009) p. 94.
17 Haas (1958) p. 127.
18 See Muller (2014).
19 Muller, J.-W. (2016) http://foreignpolicy.com/2016/03/18/angela-merkels-misunderstood-christian-mission-eu/.
20 Cited in www.euractiv.com/section/central-europe/opinion/hungary-s-turn-as-eu-president/.
21 Scruton (2013) p. 42.
22 Juncker, J. C. (2013) 'Europe's Nationalist Demons Are Only Sleeping', 12 March 2013, www.euractiv.com/section/elections/news/juncker-europe-s-nationalist-demons-are-only-sleeping.
23 Cited in *The Times*; 28 December 1992.
24 http://hungarytoday.hu/news/u2-frontman-bono-blasts-hyper-nationalist-hungary-poland-existential-threat-europe-98661.
25 Hockenos, P. (2014) 'The Government Hungarians Deserve', *Al Jazeera*, 9 April, 2014, http://america.aljazeera.com/opinions/2014/4/hungary-electionsorbanfidesznationalism.html.
26 www.spiegel.de/international/europe/a-hungarian-right-wing-extremist-explores-his-jewish-roots-a-962156.html.
27 Széky, J. (2014) 'A Tradition of Nationalism', *Eurozine*, http://www.eurozine.com/a-tradition-of-nationalism/.
28 For an example of this approach see Evans (2003) p. 6. This British historian argues that the 'unique' qualities of Hungarian nationalism 'proved highly disruptive for central Europe, indeed at times for the continent as a whole'.
29 Pack, J. 'The Hungary Model: Resurgent Nationalism', *National Interest*, 8 October 2015, http://nationalinterest.org/feature/the-hungary-model-resurgent-nationalism-14025.
30 Sugar (2000) p. 127.
31 Borsody, S. 'Hungary's Road to Trianon: Peacemaking and Propaganda', www.hungarianhistory.com/lib/tria/tria04.htm.
32 On the role of propaganda, see Borsody, S. 'Hungary's Road to Trianon: Peacemaking and Propaganda', www.hungarianhistory.com/lib/tria/tria04.htm.

33 This text is available online -https://archive.org/stream/racialproblemsin00setouoft/racialproblemsin00setouoft_djvu.txt.
34 See https://archive.org/stream/racialproblemsin00setouoft/racialproblemsin00setouoft_djvu.txt, p. 253.
35 See https://archive.org/stream/racialproblemsin00setouoft/racialproblemsin00setouoft_djvu.txt, pp. 172–173.
36 *ibid*, p. 199.
37 Seton-Watson (1911) p. 339.
38 Jeszenszky (1989) p. 154.
39 See Geehr (1990) p. 180.
40 Steed (1913) p. 169, available online https://archive.org/details/cu31924028096760.
41 Steed (1913) p. 168.
42 Kecskés (2015) p. 104.
43 Harold Nicolson (1965) p. 34.
44 Putman, J. (1983) 'Hungary's New Way – A Different Communism', National Geographic, vol. 163, no. 2, p. 253.
45 Bideleux (2015) p. 15.
46 Kis, J. (2000) 'Nation Building and Beyond', *Habitus*, no. 2, http://publications.ceu.edu/sites/default/files/publications/nation-building-and-beyond.pdf.
47 See Borsodi (1988) p. xii.
48 Vardy (1983) p. 4.
49 Vardy (1983).
50 I rely on Vardy (1983) for the translation of this excerpt from Peter, H. (1981) '"Viszonylagos Nemzettudat' (Relative National Consciousness)', *Elet es Irodalom (Life and Literature)*, vol. 25, no. 20, 25 July 1981, pp. 4–5.
51 Cited in the *Frankfurter Rundschau*; 14 January 1987.
52 See the discussion in Rabinbach (1988)
53 Cited in Eley (1988) p. 196.
54 See Risse & Engelmann-Martin (2002)
55 Pänke (2015) p. 354.
56 Pänke (2015) p. 354.
57 Márai (2000).
58 1993 De Clercq report on communication file:///Users/frankfuredi/Documents/2016/EU%20hist%20value/DE_CLERCQ_REPORT_INFO._COMM._POLICY.pdf
59 Della Sala (2016) p. 524.
60 Shore (2000) p. 58.
61 Martín-Arroyo (2014) p. 14.
62 Martín-Arroyo (2014) p. 10.
63 See Foret & Littoz-Monnet p. 20.
64 Beck (2005) p. 230.
65 Beck (2005) p. 234.
66 Beck, U. & Giddens, A. 'Nationalism Has become the Enemy of Europe's Nations', *The Guardian*, 4 October 2005.
67 Habermas (2016) pp. 48–49.
68 Muller (2016) p. 3.
69 Muller (2016) p. 28.
70 See Mueller, J.-W. (2016) 'A Majority of "Deplorables"', 10 November 2016, www.project-syndicate.org/commentary/trump-voters-opposition-to-democracy-by-jan-werner-mueller-2016-11.
71 Müller (2007) p. 30.
72 Muller (2007) p. 2.
73 Muller (2007) p. 9.
74 Baumeister (2007) p. 483.
75 Baumeister (2007) p. 485.
76 Beck & Grande (2007) p. 54.

77 Beck & Grande (2007) p. 53.
78 Beck, U. (2007) 'A New Cosmopolitanism in the Air', *SignandSight.Com*, 20 November/ 2007, www.signandsight.com/features/1603.html.
79 Bibo (1976).
80 Cited in *The Daily Telegraph*, 11 July 2007, www.telegraph.co.uk/news/worldnews/1557143/ Barroso-hails-the-European-empire.html.
81 Müller, J.-W. (2013) *Safeguarding Democracy Inside the EU Brussels and the Future of Liberal Order Transatlantic*, Academy Paper Series, February 2013, p. 13.
82 Cited in Egeddy (2013).
83 Wilkin (2016) p. 84.
84 Della Sala (2016) p. 524.
85 Meier (2005) pp. 18–19.

4

MEMORY WARS OR THE CRUSADE AGAINST THE PAST

It is very difficult to entirely ignore the past. But since the 1980s, Western culture has exhibited a discernible attempt to decouple the present from the past. In part this trend is fuelled by a palpable sense of Western society's estrangement from its historical legacy, which transcends the conventional ideological divide. From radical postmodernism to mainstream liberal and conservative thought, the West has become emotionally disconnected from the past. Thus in reference to racist incidents in football, the former British Conservative prime minister, David Cameron, could declare in February 2012 that 'we will not let recent events drag us back to the bad old days of the past'.[1] His use of the phrase 'bad old days' constituted more than a response to a single ugly incident.

Unease towards the legacy of the past is even more pronounced within leftist and liberal opinion. That scepticism towards the relevance of the legacy of the past unites virtually all sections of the Western intelligentsia was strikingly affirmed by Gareth Stedman Jones, a former member of the editorial board of the *New Left Review*, when he wrote:

> The once magical invocation of history's numinous and redemptive powers now looks either tawdry or sinister. From Passchendaele to Auschwitz, from the Gulag to Hiroshima, and so on to the Killing Fields, the twentieth century has remorselessly torn away from us all remaining vestiges of a simple nineteenth century faith in progress.[2]

Not all accounts of the past are as negative as Stedman Jones'; but within Western popular and high culture alike, positive accounts of a nation's history are conspicuously rare. The usage of the term 'Victorian values' or 'Victorian morality' in Britain often conveys the connotation of narrow-minded and bigoted attitudes, a rigid social code of conduct, an unhealthy culture of sexual restraint, and the scandal of child labour.

The metaphor of the 'bad old days' is often deployed as a useful corrective to the supposed nostalgia of populism. Anti-populist commentators often ridicule the targets of their polemic as simple and gullible people who, unlike them, actually believe that the past possesses some redeeming features. 'Populists will pine for an imaginary, whitewashed past until politicians offer a credible future,' asserts Cas Mudde of the University of Georgia.[3] The critique of nostalgia does not merely caution people about the problem of living in the past: it also seeks to de-legitimate the values and customs that prevailed yesteryear. Mudde, who accuses populists of whitewashing the past, appears to be unaware of his own impulse to represent it as an unending story of oppression and hypocrisy. The outcome of the cultural war against the past is to morally distance society from its history.

Some historians have gone so far as to claim that the people of Europe have become psychically distanced from the past to such an extent that they no longer need history to cultivate their identity or to make sense of who they are. 'Clearly Europeans have a sense of themselves as survivors of a history they have left far behind them; they do not see history as their origin or the foundation on which they stand', argues Meier. He adds:

> History is not something they desire to carry on (in a better way if possible). Hence they feel no gratitude to their forebears for what they achieved with so much labor; on the contrary, they are fixated on all the things they don't understand (and are making an effort to understand), such as wars, injustice, discrimination against women, slavery, and the like. They feel uncoupled from their history, the seriousness of which they are, generally speaking, less and less able to imagine.[4]

As evidence of this trend, Meier cites the EU's attempt to detach itself from Europe's historical past: 'Thus, as far as I can see, the European Union is emerging as the first political entity of the modern era that has no need for its own history and for a historical orientation'.[5]

Up to a point, Meier is right to highlight the tendency of advocates of European federalism to detach the societies of the continent from their national history. To a significant extent, the project of European unification was driven by an understandable impulse to start afresh and leave the 'bad old days' behind. However, not even an institution like the EU could expect the citizens of Europe to identify with it without drawing on the authority of history. And certainly since the 1980s, the past has become an important issue for the EU. In order to strengthen its authority, the EU has sought to exploit the resources provided by history to legitimate its institutions. Its politics of memory are inextricably linked to the values that the EU acclaims as its own. Yet the politics of memory often provoke conflict – there is more than one version of the past, and the stories promoted by the EU often contradict those advocated by other groups, parties, and nations that inhabit the European continent.

As we argue in this chapter, the EU's narrative of the past fundamentally contradicts the way that Hungary and some of the other Eastern European nations deal with their history. Indeed, the cultural conflicts that we explored in previous chapters are closely linked to this contradictory approach towards the past. This difference in approach is most strikingly expressed in the contrasting emotional tone and attitude towards history: in the case of the EU, it is one of an embarrassed alienation, whereas in Hungary it is one of respect. This memory war is also directly linked to contrasting attitudes to the nation state. In the case of Hungary, the politics of memory are directed towards the mobilization of resources that support the authority of its status as a sovereign nation, and against the non-national political culture that was institutionalized during the communist dictatorship. Inevitably the reaction against its previous non-national and anti-patriotic memory regime assumes a national form. In contrast, EU historiography is drawn towards the promotion of a transnational, even anti-national, representation of the past.

The memory wars raging between Hungary and partisans of the EU can also be interpreted as revolving around the question of who gets to decide the meaning of the past. The issue of the relationship of the past to Hungarian identity was suspended during the Stalinist era – precisely the time that the EU was busy elaborating its transnational version of history. So while Hungarians were acutely conscious that they had been dispossessed of their past, which some experienced as a loss of their patrimony, EU-phile commentators and historians were busy minimizing the relevance of national histories to contemporary life.

As it turned out, after the regime change in Hungary, the anti-nationalist version of history favoured by the ideologues of the EU directly contradicted many of the traditions that underpin attempts to constitute Hungary's national identity and that of large parts of East Europe. In their quest for legitimacy, upholding their respective view of the past was, and remains, essential for both parties in order to affirm their authority.

The politicization of history

There is little doubt that in Hungary and large parts of East Europe, history has become an important terrain for cultural contestation. Such debates centre on competing claims about the status of different symbols of nationhood, contrasting interpretations of historical events and which historical figures should be acclaimed or castigated. The most controversial topic of debate in Hungary is the question of how the period between 1918–1945 should be assessed and memorialized, followed by controversies over how the communist era ought to be evaluated. As one critic of the politicization of history noted, the 'expression "emlékezetpolitika" – memory politics – has returned to the Hungarian language, and is used to qualify political actions which, following a specific agenda, attempt to use political memory as a way of forming shared identity and of influencing the behaviour of voters'.[6]

One striking manifestation of the politicization of memory in Hungary is the number of disputes surrounding the renaming of streets and the initiatives to erect statues honouring right-wing and, in some cases, anti-Semitic nationalist politicians from the interwar era, such as Bálint Hóman and György Donáth. There have also been heated exchanges about the removal of statues from public places. Kossuth Square, just outside the Parliament building in Budapest, has seen the removal of the statues of two historical figures: Mihály Károlyi, a former prime minister, and the poet Attila Jozsef. There have been constant disputes about the siting of a memorial to the victims of the Second World War in Freedom Square in Budapest. Opponents of this memorial complain that the memorial simply points the finger at Germany for the horrors afflicted on the nation during the Second World War and absolves Hungarian collaborators of responsibility for the war crimes that were perpetuated in this era. Hungary's role during the Second World War, the significance of the Holocaust, the legacy of the communist dictatorship, the meaning of Trianon, and the question of how the 1956 Revolution should be remembered are recurrent themes in Hungary's memory wars.

Numerous Western commentators take the view that the preoccupation of East European nations such as Hungary with their past is qualitatively different from the more rational, future-oriented practices of Western societies. But such ethno-centric perceptions of Hungarian memory politics fail to account for the fact that the EU has devoted considerable resources towards promoting a historical narrative that legitimates its existence. In the 1990s, it sponsored the publication of an ill-fated European history textbook for use in schools throughout the continent.[7] Its public relations campaigns, which were designed to invent a new narrative for the EU, recognized the importance of historical memory as a source of legitimacy: the *New Narrative for Europe* project was based on the premise that a 'common history is obviously the main source of collective identity for a community'.[8] The EU's most ambitious attempt to influence the cultivation of a European memory is the yet-to-be completed House of European History project in Brussels. As one account of the 'Politics of Remembrance at the House of European History' observed, 'the past 25 years have seen a veritable boom in historical museums and exhibitions in Europe'.[9]

Many studies indicate that since the 1980s, the EU has become increasingly devoted to developing a version of history that can provide the foundation for a European identity. Indeed, the more the EU has had to justify its legitimacy, the more it has sought to develop its own vision of a transnational past. As Oriane Calliagro argued, the 'use and overuse of the past by EU actors is a symptom of a crisis of European integration'.[10]

Despite their constant references to the past, EU actors have succeeded in deceiving themselves into believing that they are exempt from the charge of politicizing history. For example, a booklet published by the European Parliament's Socialist Group argues that: 'this abuse of the past – based on rather nationalist ideas – and other rhetoric about being truly "Polish" were echoed in similar nationalist phrases by Fidesz in Hungary and – albeit somewhat milder – by President Klaus in the Czech Republic'.[11] The booklet asserts that this 'political use of the past is against the very idea of European integration, based on peaceful cooperation without bringing up the past for political means'. EU-phile inspired commentaries often claim that, unlike East Europeans who desperately cling on to the archaic symbols of ancient times, the EU has freed itself from the burden of its past. Yet the European federalist project has always been in the business of myth-making. The use of the portrait of the Greek mythological figure of Europa on euro banknotes offers one illustration of the EU's willingness to draw on the symbols of antiquity to validate itself.

Critics of Hungary's celebration of ancient national symbols were conspicuously quiet when the EU opted to draw on the memory of the Acropolis to link its project to the 'birth' of democracy in Athens. One supporter of the instrumental use of this symbol outlined:

> In 2003, 46 years after the signature of the Rome Treaties and 14 years after the fall of the Berlin wall, the representatives of Europe's citizens were gathered in another symbolic place of Europe history, at the Acropolis in Athens – the birth place of Democracy – to celebrate the signature of the adhesion of 10 new countries to the European Union. As stressed in the declaration, this meeting was seen as 'a historical moment'.[12]

As one study explained, 'there is plenty of evidence that myth-making has been very much part of the European project and the success of integration is in some ways related to the degree to which myths have been diffused and become entrenched in political discourse and practice'.[13]

The double standard that allows Western European commentators to conveniently overlook their own society's practice of myth-making, only to deplore their Eastern neighbours' obsession with their dark past, echoes the colonial disdain towards the exotic cultures of the nineteenth century. As international relations scholar Maria Mälksoo observed:

> Orientation to the past, rather than to the future, has often been regarded as part of some putative 'East European syndrome'. Yet, this typically Orientalist approach obscures the fact that memory, as well as forgetting, is a constitutive feature of any culture or social imaginary . . . Furthermore, the claims of a 'special historicism' of East European peoples, their heightened propensity to understand the present through the past and thus to see history as a weight restraining and enabling the choices that can be made in the present, deny the extent to which the 'memory boom' has also been a firm accompaniment in Western European societies in the late twentieth and early twenty-first centuries.[14]

Of course, the memory boom flourishing in Western Europe promotes symbols, values, and ideals that are very different to those that prevail in the Eastern part of the continent. However, both parties are engaged in the practice of politicizing memory. What divides them is the kind of memory they wish people to remember and celebrate.

As suggested in previous chapters, Europe's foundational myth is based on the contrast it draws between itself and the past cultivated by national historians. Since the end of the Second World War, the central theme of the foundational narrative of European unification was its triumph over a past in which nationalist conflict threatened to destroy the continent. One study of the political myth surrounding the EU argued:

> Its basic premise is that nationalism brought the continent to the point of ruin in the twentieth century but it was in its darkest moment that the vision for a new order took root. The rise of fascism and the destruction of war were seen as the death knell of political power entrusted and enshrined in the sovereign nation state. A united Europe emerged as the response to the failures of the first half of the twentieth century. Moreover, it has been responsible for the peace and prosperity that has followed. We see a clear narrative structure in this morality tale that presents the reasons and the basis for the postwar construction of the EU.[15]

The EU's political myth is underwritten by a teleological historical philosophy that posits the European project as akin to the 'End of History'. This outlook is clearly conveyed by EU statements that convey the impression that the transition from the nation to European integration is a 'metaphysical and historical necessity'.[16] What is claimed to be a necessity for the cause of European federalism is experienced as corrosive of the national culture of some of the member states.

The divergent orientation towards the past was the topic of a speech by Viktor Orbán in October 2007. Orbán observed that Hungarians had suffered a 'major defeat' in their debate with their Western interlocutors about what constituted the main historical threat from the past and that the reason for this defeat was that Western public opinion regarded the ideologies and nationalist movements of the pre-Second World War era as the main threat to contemporary Europe, rather than that posed by the more recent experience with the communist dictatorships. Orbán stated that the focus of the West on the threat posed by the revival of xenophobic nationalism was in part a response to the outbreak of conflict in the Balkans, and he implied that preoccupation with the return of pre-war nationalism meant that the West underestimated the far more urgent task of settling scores with the legacy of the communist dictatorship.[17] Evidently the contrasting historical experiences of these two regions of Europe has not only encouraged mutual misunderstanding but also created divergent demands on the past.

Divergent demands on the past

A preoccupation with the politics of memory transcends the cultural gulf between the different protagonists disputing the past. What divides them is a fundamental difference in how historical memory is perceived and used, a divide between the impulse to settle scores with the past and the impulse to break away from it.

In its most dramatic form, post-nationalist theoreticians call for the disavowal of the past and for a thoroughgoing break with everything that occurred before 1945. Their disavowal of the past does not mean that they are not interested in the politics of memory: on the contrary, they constantly iterate the gory details of history, such as slavery and the Holocaust, and instrumentally deploy them as cautionary tales against their ideological foes. The refrain 'it is just like the 1930s' serves as a front-line rhetorical weapon to discipline those who defy transnational conventions. The main target is the affirmation of historical continuity, which is often justified on the grounds that after the Holocaust, appeals to the legacy of the past and to histori-cal continuity must be cast aside. This proposition is most forcefully asserted by Habermas, for whom a total break from 'historical life' is an ethical imperative. He warned that:

> Auschwitz has become the signature of an entire epoch – and thus con-cerns all of us. Something happened there that no one could previously have thought possible. It touched a deep layer of solidarity among all who wear a human face. Until then – despite the monstrosities of world history – we had simply taken the integrity of this deep layer for granted. A band of naivete was torn to shreds at Auschwitz – a naivete from which unquestioning tradi-tions had drawn their authority, from which historical continuities in general had lived. Auschwitz altered the conditions for the continuation of historical life – and not only in Germany.[18]

At first sight, the anti-humanist thesis proposed by Habermas appears as a thought-ful attempt to draw attention to the singular significance of the Holocaust. But on closer inspection, his endeavour to turn the Holocaust into a secular version of original sin turns this tragedy into a moralistic exhortation for constituting a new form of personhood. Habermas' narrative of the Fall of Men demands that people not only renounce their past but also their traditions, nationality, and history. The principal target of this narrative is the consciousness of historical continuity.

The adoption of a post-nationalist attitude towards history has far less appeal in the East than in Western Europe. To be sure, sections of the Eastern European intel-ligentsia have expressed an affinity towards post-nationalist culture and history. In Hungary, intellectuals who perceived themselves as Westernized liberals have often found it difficult to relate to popular national sentiments. For example, the Hungar-ian dissident George Konrad is, like Habermas, bitterly hostile to ideas that support the sovereignty of nationhood. In his book *Antipolitics*, he put his faith in the leading role of an 'international intelligentsia' and expressed a preference for his identity as a European over all else. He claimed that 'what is most important today . . . is to emancipate thinking people from the narrow vision of national teamwork under state auspices and to engage in a dialogue high above the level of governments and national boundaries'.[19]

Because of their estrangement from the *demos*, Konrad, like some of his intellec-tual colleagues in the democratic opposition to the communist Regime in the 1970s and 1980s, even looked upon the 1956 Hungarian Revolution with ambivalence, regarding 'uncontrolled mass movements' with disdain and feeling more at home with 'patient' cosmopolitan intellectuals.[20] The historian Miklós Szabò, in an essay titled 'An Embarrassing Revolution' (1991), observes that in the aftermath of 1956, in private conversations amongst the Hungarian intelligentsia, the consensus was that if there had been no revolution the nation would have progressed far further along the path of de-Stalinization.[21] The logic of this perspective led to the conclusion that it was far better to forget the 1956 Revolution than to memorialize it.

This attitude of embarrassment towards the events of 1956 was, and remains, symptomatic of a reluctance to come to terms with the oppressive regime that dominated Hungary between 1948 and 1989. It also serves as testimony of an alienated sensibility and psychic distance from the single most important expression of popular aspiration for freedom in the history of post-war Hungary. Since the 1956 Revolution is the anti-populist's nightmare, their reaction to this mass movement for freedom is understandable.

Even sources that are sympathetic to the outlook of the Hungarian liberal intelligentsia acknowledge that this group is wedded to an elitist and anti-popular sensibility.[22] The reluctance of this section of society to settle scores with the experience of the communist dictatorship contributed to the evasion of confronting Hungary's troublesome past during the negotiations surrounding regime change and in the immediate period that followed. For a while, it appeared that issues thrown up in Hungary's past would become minor questions of interest only to a small group of professional historians. However, this hesitant de-politicization of Hungary's past could not endure for long.

The negative legacy of the Stalinist era could not disappear overnight, and its injustices weighed heavily on the outlook of a significant section of Hungarian society. In such circumstances, it was inevitable that any serious attempt to confront this legacy would raise the question of what it means to be a Hungarian – and the very posing of this question would lead to a renewed interest in nationhood and national history. Consequently, the years following regime change in Hungary saw the emergence of the politics of national revival and the attempt to find meaning in the nation's history.

National revival in Hungary emerged as a reaction to the anti-nationalist, or denationalized, political culture of the communist era. As one British academic explained, 'across the "national" camp' as a whole, Hungarian nationhood is 'now constructed primarily against communism', adding that, 'like many other post-communist nation builders and state builders, therefore, Hungary's "national" camp sees itself as seeking to overturn the communist legacy'.[23] Unfortunately, some Western commentators interpreted Hungary's national revival as proof that the dangerous force that wreaked havoc in the 1930s had returned to haunt Europe. From this perspective, the very attempt to mobilize Hungary's memory to cultivate its national identity was perceived as a challenge to the post-national ethos that informed their worldview.

National revival in Hungary coincided with the rise of powerful anti-national currents in Western European historiography. From the 1980s onwards, even the slightest interest in national history was treated with suspicion and in some circles 'national history' was condemned as an accomplice to xenophobic politics. 'We, historians, need to reflect on how to deal with national histories especially after they have demonstrated to be so dangerous in the past by legitimating wars and genocides,' argued one of its opponents.[24] Historians such as Stefan Berger portray national histories as a dangerous virus that needs to be contained. Berger has argued that such a containment strategy demands that the 'naturalisation' and 'essentialisation' of national narratives should be forcefully 'denaturalised and 'de-essentialised' in order to reduce the harms they can cause. He also asserted that the threat posed by national history should be limited by the creation of 'kaleidoscopic national histories' that recast national memory into multiple diverse fragments.[25]

EU-phile critics of the construction of national historical narratives rightly point out that memory is sometimes manipulated in order to manufacture a glorious golden age and a heroic national past. Yet they are no less committed to inventing a past that flatters their vision of a post-national, transnational, kaleidoscopic, cosmopolitan world. Whatever the defects of national histories, they pale into insignificance when compared to the propagandist project of fabricating a shared European memory and a common European history.

Some of the supporters of the project to construct a shared European memory explicitly acknowledge the instrumental and artificial character of their scheme. The French EU-phile political scientist Fabrice Larat, an enthusiastic proponent of this endeavour, wrote that the 'instrumentalization of the past for means of legitimization and community-building is not restricted to nation states'.[26] For Larat, the instrumentalization of the past is an essential precondition for ensuring that all members of the EU sign up to what he characterized as an '*Acquis historique communautaire*' – a historical memory that communicates 'a shared belief about the historical purpose of the common system of governance that is now the EU'.[27] The objective of an *acquis historique communautaire* was to ensure that the values of the project of European unification are underpinned by a common narrative of history. Larat's version of the past is based on distilling references to history from the technical and legal documents drawn up during the course of European unification. He asserts that:

> The core values of European integration expressed in the leading narratives of the history of European integration have, with time, been crystallised into a corpus of guiding principles and soft norms implicitly intended to conduct the politics of the Union. They are all related to the official interpretation of the past and build together the historically based objectives of European unification.[28]

The perfunctory appeals to history in the preambles to EU official documents have an essentially rhetorical character. Stringing them together into an *acquis historique communautaire* simply highlights the artificiality of this enterprise. What Larat offers is a policy-led history dictated by the demand for a common European memory.

The instrumentalization of the past by the partisans of a shared European memory is essentially an administrative exercise conducted through technocratic practices. This is a public relations campaign, which Shore well described as a 'characteristically top-down, managerial and instrumental approach to "culture building"'.

Shore rightly questioned 'its assumption that "European identity" can somehow be engineered from above and injected into the masses by an enlightened vanguard of European policy professionals using the latest communication technologies and marketing techniques'.[29]

The project of Europeanizing memory has relied on administrative fiat and the rewriting of history. It depends, not on the elaboration of a sophisticated or subtle historiography, but on its institutional power to subject EU member states to political and cultural pressure to denationalize their past. According to the vision projected by partisans of the Europeanization of memory, the interpretation of the past becomes a shared enterprise in a post-national Europe. Their aim is to underwrite economic and political harmonization with the coordination of historical memory. Attempts to promote common memory laws on Holocaust denial or the denial of the Armenian Genocide illustrate some of the initiatives undertaken to institutionalize the Europeanization of memory.

Schemes designed to rewrite history textbooks and to promote transnational historiography at the expense of national ones are regular themes in the EU's memory war. The EC's financial support for historical research is influenced by its political objectives and consequently, as one recipient of its largesse noted, 'academic selection criteria were not strictly applied'.[30] Oriane Calliagro's study of the EU's research policy concluded that this institution 'actively encouraged deterritorialised and teleological histories of Europe while simultaneously worrying that by doing so it replicated the efforts of so-called "totalitarian" states to rewrite history'.[31]

One commentary on the EU's attempt to Europeanize memory concluded that 'the aspiration to use history to foster a postnational European identity is problematic'.[32] It is simply too difficult to construct a version of historical memory that would satisfy all the member states. An example of the challenge faced by transnational memory entrepreneurs is illustrated by the failure of the EU's 'A New Narrative for Europe' project. This project was charged by the EC, during 2013–2014, with the task of framing a new narrative about shared history and values in order to create a 'transnational memory in Europe'.[33] One of the project's aims was to provide a 'strong historical perspective', and the managers of this initiative demanded 'a common framework of shared stories'. However the participants of this project found it difficult to come up with any compelling shared stories. In face of disagreement about the meaning of the past, the commission was forced to change its terminology from 'narrative' to narratives'.[34]

The divergent demands on the past are unlikely to be overcome through compromise or diplomatic negotiation. The most significant division on this matter corresponds to the contrasting historical experience of East and West Europe. This point is clearly recognized by supporters of the Europeanization of memory, such as Larat:

> When debating about the virtues of nationalism in the light of EU-integration, a line of demarcation seems to run through Europe between citizens of Western countries on the one hand and those from Central and Eastern European

countries on the other. This particularly holds true in combination with interpretation of the past as part of national and of what could be our common European identity. Collective memories in Europe after the eastern enlargement are split up and by far not always consensual. The dark shadows of Europe's pasts that are the memories of wars, military occupation, genocides and totalitarianism obviously represent a new kind of invisible but omnipresent wall dividing the continent. This historical curtain is made up of misunderstandings, prejudices, and competing and conflicting memories that together lead to dissension, and sometimes to mutual accusations between EU member states.[35]

The competing and conflicting memories alluded to by Larat have encompassed a variety of different subjects. However, the most pivotal controversy over the politics of European memory hangs on the question of the relative balance between the legacy of the Holocaust and that of the Gulag.

Competing claims about the relative status of the memory of the Holocaust and the Gulag became increasingly voiced after the enlargement of the EU. As we explain in the next section, from the 1980s onwards, the memorialization of the Holocaust was transformed into the foundational normative value for the legitimation of the EU. Some of the new member states felt that their own memory of suffering under Soviet domination was neglected by the unique significance attached to the Holocaust in the EU's politics of memory. Substantive political debates about the past were not possible during the course of the EU membership negotiation process. As one study of this 'Potemkin Europeanization' noted, 'EU pressure' in Hungary 'stifled the *"Kulturkampf"* between so-called 'westernisers' and 'traditionalists'.[36] However the conflicting approaches to the nation's past soon came to the surface. Larat observed in 2008 that the 'memory of the Holocaust which has been a core element of the *"acquis historique communautaire"* until now is challenged by other dramatic experiences from the past such as communism or national memories that are object to conflicting interpretations in different parts of the EU'.[37]

It is to the questions raised by the Europeanization of memory through the medium of the Holocaust that we now turn.

When does history begin?

In the midst of the prominent role that memory politics achieved in twenty-first century European culture, it is easy to overlook the fact that the sacralisation of the Holocaust played a relatively minor role in the early phase of European unification. In the 1940s and 1950s, European federalist propagandists had not yet assigned the memory of the Holocaust its current pivotal role. As one study recalled, 'post 1945 West European societies relied very much on the myth of resistance'; the memory of the Holocaust was portrayed as a variant of the 'victimization' suffered by nations such as Austria, Belgium or Holland'.[38] In the 1940s and 1950s, the main emphasis of the European federalist version of the past was to draw a moral contrast between its vision of the future and the grim events that led to the outbreak of two world wars. The new Europe's foundational narrative was based on the drawing of a moral contrast between itself and the destructive politics of nationalism. The image of a disunited and conflict-ridden old Europe served as the negative counterpoint to a unified and harmonious post-national continent.

The narrative that emerged in the 1950s told of a tale of how the original member states of the EU emerged, phoenix-like, from the ashes of the war to renounce nationalism as a basis for conducting relations between states. According to this version of events, European unity was responsible for transcending the nationalist conflicts that had led to numerous wars and also for creating the conditions for economic prosperity in the post-Second World War decades. From this standpoint, the achievement of European unity was portrayed as a secular equivalent of historic redemption. In this story, European federalism symbolized a sacred cause, while nationalism was assigned the role of anti-Christ.

One of the unfortunate consequences of this myth of redemption was that it went beyond the renunciation of the dark era of 1914–1945 to repudiate much of the past. Europe's pre-1945 past was increasingly depicted in negative terms. In part, this attitude was a reaction to the abuse of history by politically motivated nationalist historians during the previous two centuries. It also expressed the concern that dwelling too closely on the pre-1945 era would exacerbate conflict between member states and other European nations. The EU's cultural and educational initiatives consequently peddled a simplistic account of history that made little attempt to educate people to understand the legacy of European civilization. Young people embarking on the study of the past could easily gain the conviction that Europe was born in the aftermath of 1945.

For the EU educational establishment, the history of the continent before 1946 is an alien, hostile territory. Take for example *The EU Explained: A Toolkit for Teachers*, published by the London-based Hansard Society.[39] This toolkit is entirely focused on providing pupils with an understanding of the EU's institutional framework. Its underlying objective is to outline advantages of being a member of the EU; it offers no insight into what it means to be a European and contains only one very short paragraph that touches on the historical legacy of the continent:

> After the Second World War, the countries of Europe were left devastated and they were determined not to let such destruction happen again. Europe began thinking of ways in which future conflict could be prevented.[40]

An inspection of the educational resources on this subject indicate that *The EU Explained* is typical of a tendency to discuss Europe outside of any historical, philosophical or, indeed, intellectual context.[41] The end of the Second World War marks the beginning of all that is good.

Year Zero history has been instrumentalized to work as a cautionary tale regarding the dangerous consequences of seeking a national solution to social and economic problems. During the Eurozone crisis of 2010–2013, leading EU representatives, like

Herman van Rompuy, often warned that if his institution were to fail, 'the spectre of nationalism and war would once again reign over the continent'.[42] In a speech marking the fall of the Berlin Wall, Van Rompuy stated, echoing François Mitterand: 'Le nationalisme, c'est la guerre'.[43]

Periodic attempts to dig deeper into Europe's past and draw on its legacy are quickly abandoned because of apprehensions about the divisions that they are likely to provoke between member states. The debate on the Draft Treaty for establishing a constitution for Europe in 2004 illustrates this danger. Politicians from different parties and nations clashed on the question of whether Christianity should be evoked in the document as part of Europe's heritage. Following a long debate, the authors decided not to include a reference to Christianity in the Preamble to the constitutional document.[44] From the standpoint of Year Zero history, erasing Christianity from Europe's official memory is a small price to pay for avoiding coming to terms with a complicated past.

Although the EU's advocacy of 1945 as Year Zero history avoids having to deal with messy conflicts, such a negative vision does little to inspire people. It also fails to confront the question of how to construct a focus for a transnational European memory. The salience of this issue was recognized in the late 1970s when it became evident to EU policymakers that it was necessary to tackle the question of how to motivate people to develop a sense of European identity. Numerous scholars contend that from the 1990s onwards, the Holocaust was increasingly perceived 'as having the potential to become the EU's definitional myth'.[45] By definitional myth, Littoz-Monnett meant 'a narrative chosen by a given society in order to explain how it came about and who it is. In other words, a definitional myth provides societies with a story about their origins and a basis for the definition of their identity'.[46]

One of the consequences of the adoption of the Holocaust as the EU's definitional myth was that it was transformed into an ahistorical, transcendent sacred experience. The sacralization of the Holocaust initially evolved in Western European societies in the 1990s. In these countries, memory work on Nazi crimes had acquired an unprecedented degree of momentum and influence. Whereas in the early phase of European unification, the genocide directed at European Jews was 'scarcely a point of reference', by the 1990s the Holocaust became a central theme of EU-supported memory work. From then on, however, EU elites within the European Parliament and the EC began referring to the Holocaust as the tragic event that changed the values of European societies. As Klas-Göran Karlsson explains in his study of this process, 'to date the best example of a canonisation of history in the name of the European dimension is the case of the Holocaust'.[47]

EU statements about how the values of European societies had changed in light of the Holocaust were rarely rendered explicit. However, in practice this implied a willingness to repudiate Europe's past and the values with which it was traditionally associated. Müller spelled out this approach when he claimed that the repudiation of the past by the EU might provide that foundation for a new form of political legitimacy.[48] European federalists used the threat of a possible descent in to the horrors of the Holocaust as a warning against the critics of their project. For example, in a Victory Day speech in Thereisienstadt in 2005, the Swedish EU commissioner and the then vice president of the European Community, Margot Wallström, told her audience that the Second World War was caused by greedy nationalists, that the EU was founded to eliminate such evils, and that Eurosceptics risked a 'return to the Holocaust'.[49] The ease with which Wallström made the conceptual leap from Euroscepticism and to the spectre of an impending Holocaust demonstrated the usefulness of the canonization of this tragic genocide.

It was during the 1990s that the EU took steps to initiate the project of Europeanizing the memory of the Holocaust. EU heritage policies became increasingly devoted towards deploying resources to the memorialization of the victims of Nazi crimes. The Holocaust was more and more evoked as an all-purpose warning against the dangers of all forms of nationalism.

On 21 June 1995, the European Parliament unanimously agreed to launch a Holocaust memorial day in all the member states. The different EU institutions promoted the memorialization of the Holocaust as a sacred duty from which no member state could opt out. As one study pointed out, resolutions passed by the European Parliament obliged would-be East European member states to sign up to its definitional myth. It noted that, in effect, 'candidate EU states were asked to perform their duty of "coping with their past", either as perpetrators of or accomplices to racist crimes committed during World War II, before they could join the EU'.[50] The suitability of candidate states like Hungary was to be judged on this point. Müller argued that the Holocaust had become a 'test case' of the liberal-democratic morality for East European countries.[51]

As we will see, the *de facto* issuing of such an ultimatum was unlikely to win hearts and minds. In the long run the elevation of the Holocaust into the core value of official EU dogma actually undermined the authentic and genuine attempts to give meaning to this unique tragedy.

The authors of the canonization of the Holocaust shamelessly promoted the rewriting of history. For example Beate Winkler, former director of the *European Monitoring Centre on Racism and Xenophobia*, explained to her audience at a conference of the Organisation for Security and Co-operation (OSCE) in Europe in June 2005 that 'the Shoah is the traumatic experience of Europe's recent history; it has driven the EU's founders to build a united and peaceful Europe, and thus been at the very root of the European integration project'.[52] European integration based on the need to regulate conflict between Germany and France, the exigencies of the Cold War, and the demands of the Marshall Plan was cynically reinterpreted as a therapeutic initiative designed to come to terms with the traumatic experience of the Shoah.

One of the consequences of the sacralization of the Holocaust was that it became torn from its historical context and turned into a preachy morality play that could be opportunistically used to assist the cause of forging a shared European memory. A former European commissioner for Research, Innovation and Science, Máire Geoghegan Quinn, justified the teaching of the Holocaust on the grounds that it was a 'good way to have future generations understand the importance of fundamental rights, which are one of the central pillars of "European" citizenship"'.[53] Her exhortation to adopt the Holocaust as a useful teaching aid illustrates the instrumental and fundamentally political use to which its memory was put.

The Gulag memory versus the Shoah memory

Although the sacralization of the Holocaust continues to play a key role in the memory politics of the EU, its singular moral authority has come under question in recent years. In part this has been caused by Holocaust fatigue – the constant appeal to the authority of this memory has encouraged some to adopt the attitude of 'I don't want to hear about this anymore'. More importantly, many of the new East European member states of the EU inevitably reacted to the expectation that they had little choice but to subordinate their concern to settle scores with their communist past to the imperative of commemorating the Holocaust. Political leaders throughout the post-Soviet world argued that the failure to assign the crimes of Soviet domination the same moral status as the evils committed by the Nazis was manifestly unfair. As Laure Neumayer remarked, 'anti-Communist activists set out to fight against what they perceived as the 'double standards' in the political, moral, and legal judgment of Nazism and Stalinism'.[54]

One of the consequences of the EU's Eastern enlargement was that from 2004 onwards, 'the status of the Holocaust as the definitional myth of the European project started to be debated'.[55] Eastern European states often took exception to the minor and undistinguished role that was assigned to their distinct experience in EU memory politics, and they articulated an alternative version of European memory 'according to which Nazi and Stalinist crimes are comparable and should, as such, occupy an equally significant place in EU commemoration and identity policies'.[56] Their arguments, put forward in different venues, were based on a historical interpretation that highlighted 'the equivalence of the two "totalitarianisms", Stalinism and Nazism'. It 'directly challenged the prevailing Western European narrative constructed on the uniqueness of the Holocaust as the epitome of evil'.[57]

The principal objective of East European memory entrepreneurs was the demand that the EU recognize 'more explicitly the sufferings endured by the "other Europe" under Nazi occupation and Communism'.[58] The equivalence that they drew between the crimes of the Nazi and Stalinist regimes called into question 'the singularity of the Holocaust as the crime against humanity of the twentieth century'.[59] One of the lamentable consequences of this attempt to gain recognition for the injustices suffered under Stalinist domination was to give weight to the trend towards the relativization of the Holocaust.

The challenge to the EU's definitional myth gained significant headway during the years 2007–2010. For example, a conference on 'European Conscience and Communism' organized by the Czech Institute of National Memory in June 2008 resulted in a declaration that insisted that 'the moral, political, and legal treatment of Communism be placed on a par with that of Nazism'.[60] The 'Prague Declaration on European Conscience and Totalitarianism' was endorsed by numerous dissidents such as Va´clav Havel, Joachim Gauck, and Vytautas Landsbergis and by 50 members of the European Parliament. Although the resolution stated that the Nazi and communist totalitarian regimes should 'each be judged by their own terrible merits', the text stressed the 'substantial similarities' between them.[61]

The cumulative effect of the campaign to alter the EU's memory politics was the adoption of the 'Resolution on European Conscience and Totalitarianism' by the European Parliament on 2 April 2009. During the debates that led up the adoption of this resolution, numerous representatives of the new member states insisted that as matters stood, their nations were excluded from the memory of Europe. Arguing against what was perceived as a double standard in the approach to the management of the communist and Nazi legacies, the Hungarian MEP, Lászlo Tökés, stated:

> The European Community must abandon the double standard that is evident in the different ways in which Nazism and Communism have been judged. Both inhumane dictatorships deserve equal condemnation. I ask the European Parliament to stand in solidarity with the victims of Fascist Communism and to help defeat the enduring legacy of Communism in accordance with the aforementioned moral, historical and political exigencies. Only in this way can a divided Europe be truly unified.[62]

The passing of the Resolution on 'European Conscience and Totalitarianism' represented a concession to the aspiration of some of the new member states to have their experience of victimization recognized.

Mälksoo wrote of the 'memorial militancy' of the 'new Europeans', whose emphasis on communist crimes had an unsettling impact on their Western counterpart. It is important to note that this memorial militancy was also directed at the domestic political scene, where anti-communist politicians and commentators took exception to the fact that their opponents were not forced to take responsibility for their actions before regime change. Many of the memorial militants believed that as a result of the careful management of regime change and the accession process to the EU, former leaders and beneficiaries of the old regimes were let off the hook. From their perspective, a recalibration of their national memory was necessary not only to set right the historical record but also to settle the score with the still influential members of the old *nomenklatura*.

Inevitably 'the upsurge of World War II-related memories in the East has thus often been regarded as obstructing the progress of the European project'.[63] It became evident that the 'new states did not identify with the EU's discourse on the Holocaust and attempted to impose their own memory narrative'.[64] What these debates indicated was that the reliance of the EU on the Holocaust as its definitional myth could no longer work as an unquestioned, taken-for-granted source for a European memory.

Some commentators have characterized the campaign to establish a relationship of equivalence between the crimes of the Nazi and Stalinist regimes as an attempt to set the '"Gulag memory" against a "Shoah" memory'.[65] One of the unfortunate consequences of this process of competitive claims-making was to encourage a binary, zero-sum conception of the relationship between the crimes of Nazism and Stalinism. During the course of the debate it often appeared that some believed that affording the crimes of Stalinism serious recognition would diminish the value of the memory of the Holocaust. At the same time, the implication that the resources devoted to the memorialization of the Holocaust would necessarily be at the expense of giving due recognition of the crimes of Stalinism was also frequently conveyed.

The main loser of this zero-sum view of the past was a sense of history that placed both of these tragedies in their proper historical context and tried to make sense of them as catastrophes in their own right. The fact that the tension between the Gulag and the Shoah memories is not just the product of regional differences between East and West Europe, but often also corresponds to conflicts of view between left and right, ensures that the memory wars over these two events are far from resolved. Instead of genuinely acknowledging the suffering that both of these tragedies imposed on humanity, the politicization of memory has unleashed a mean spirited process of competitive claims-making.

The quest for historical continuity

Although competing claims about the relative status of the Gulag and the Holocaust often overshadow discussions on the politics of memory in Europe, arguably more fundamental questions tend to be overlooked. Ultimately the most important issue at stake in these controversies is whether or not national communities can imagine themselves as the embodiments of some form of historical community. Although communities can be formed voluntaristically, existing nations need to be able to situate their understanding of themselves in relation to events in the past. Year Zero historiography seeks to displace this need by offering a negative version of history, where people's identity is supposedly forged through a common affirmation of writing off the past as a series of terrible events. It is what the historian Henry Rousso has characterized as 'negative history'.[66]

The Roman philosopher Cicero understood far more about the relationship between history and human development than promoters of the Year Zero approach to Europe's past, when he stated that 'not to know what has been transacted in former times is to continue always a child'. Without a sense of continuity of history, many people feel disoriented. They also intuit that they have lost their national distinctiveness. 'After the Second World War, slowly, we became grey,' argued Orbán at the National Image Conference in December 1999.[67] A grey, non-descript, and non-historical world would be all too familiar to any sensitive individual who has lived through the Stalinist era in Hungary. The aspiration for a sense of distinctiveness linked to the sensibility of historical continuity remains particularly important in post-communist societies.

It is worth noting that even before regime change in Hungary, groups of young populist dissidents had attempted to reconnect with their national folk culture and some of the folk music and traditions that were at risk of being lost. Since regime change, conservative nationalist movements and leaders proved to be most sensitive to this concern and have most consistently pursued the quest for historical continuity. Hungarian socialists and liberals felt estranged from such concerns and made little attempt to offer an alternative vision of Hungary's relation to its past.

The near total estrangement of the non-conservative wing of the post-Soviet Hungarian political class from the lives of the *demos* is one the most remarkable developments in the political culture of this society. Historically Hungary possessed a tradition of leftist populism. Prominent populist intellectuals like István Bibo, Mihaly Babits, and Laszlo Német had a natural affinity towards national concerns. Today, when the Hungarian left regards the concern with the injustices of the Treaty of Trianon as a right-wing cause, it is well worth recalling the poem 'No, No Never' that Attila Jozsef (1905–1937) wrote in 1922. 'No, No, Never' was a nationalist slogan that was widely used by Hungarians concerned with the dismemberment of their nation, and it articulated their determination not to accept this humiliating treaty. To this day, the slogan symbolizes an aspiration for the reunification of all Hungarians. Attila Jozsef enthusiastically endorsed this sentiment and in his poem pledged that Hungarians would rather die than abandon their historical heritage. Yet this poet was far from being a right-wing nationalist: he possessed a radical social conscience that eventually led him to join the illegal Hungarian Communist Party in 1930. His poetry often conveyed a powerful mood of anger and bitterness about the plight of the poor and the absence of social justice.

During the Stalinist era, Attila Jozsef was treated as a national icon and as the leading representative of Hungarian proletarian poetry. But the Stalinist cultural elite did not want the public to be acquainted with this poet's anguish about Trianon, and they attempted to extinguish his poem from the historical memory. None of the many editions of his poetry published during the Stalinist era in Hungary included his poem 'No, No Never'. It was only after regime change in 1989 that this poem was republished and rediscovered. But by this time, there were very few people on the Hungarian left who were likely to be moved by the stirring call to arms of this radical patriotic poet. It is a sad reflection of the contemporary era that Attila Joszef's poem is widely featured on the website of the far-right Jobbik Party and is unlikely to find a home on leftist media outlets.

The poem 'No, No Never' concludes with the vow that Hungary will never betray the heritage of Árpád, who was the ruler of the confederation of Hungarian tribes at the turn of the ninth and tenth centuries. It is a poem that vows to put right the injustices perpetrated through the dismemberment of Hungary by reference to the duty to preserve the nation's historical heritage. In striking contrast to this sentiment, in the course of regime change, concern with historical continuity became subordinated to the informal *acquis historique communautaire*, and a significant section of the Hungarian intelligentsia came under the influence of the EU's outlook of Year Zero history.

One of the most interesting attempts in post-regime change Hungary to counter the philosophical assumption behind the negation of historical continuity was a short essay, titled 'Conservative Manifesto' (2002), by the Hungarian neo-conservative

Straussian philosopher András Lánczi. The essay expressly addressed the question of continuity.[68] Lánczi stated that 'the foundation of every form of conservatism is namely 'preservation, conservation and the maintenance of continuity'. The problem he raised was, what did 'conservation and the maintenance of continuity' mean in the context of post-regime change Hungary?

From a classical conservative nationalist standpoint, it certainly did not mean the preservation of what Lánczi saw as the living legacy of the previous communist regime. He argued that in the current historical conjuncture, it was those people who were 'most closely connected to the old order who had something to conserve'. According to Lánczi, conservatives faced the paradox that the 'postcommunists can behave in a conservative manner while their opponents act radically'. Lánczi was reluctant to draw out the implication of his observation on this point. He warned that going down the road of radicalism was a trap which a 'genuine conservative', despite his 'legitimate passions', must avoid. Although initially, conservative nationalists adopted a hesitant approach towards the politics of memory, from 2000 onwards they wholeheartedly embraced a radical orientation towards the rehabilitation of Hungary's history through the promotion of a national revival.

As it turned out, the question of how to engage with historical continuity was not simply an issue for East European societies. For example, during the course of the attempt to draw up a *New Narrative for Europe*, it became clear that members of the committee charged with drawing up this document had very different views about the past and the meaning they derived from it. As one study of the process explains, the most important source of the controversy was over status assigned to the role of Christianity in the legacy of Europe. It noted that long-term 'historical references are far more contentious now than they were after the Second World War, especially any connections between European integration and the Christian heritage which is at odds with the prevailing inclusive political discourse'.[69] Typically the response to controversy over conflicting interpretations of the past was to minimize references to long-term historical events.

The upshot of the reluctance of the authors of the *New Narrative* to engage with the historical continuity of Europe was to provide an incoherent story, which emphasized the tragic experience of the Second World War, the fall of the Iron Curtain, and, bizarrely, the economic and financial crisis in the Eurozone. Given the arbitrary choice of these episodes, it is not surprising the declaration made 'no attempt at all to connect them'.[70]

Looking over the experience of the post-1945 era, it becomes evident that the ascendancy of Year Zero history was informed by a hesitant, often undeclared, reaction to the cultural legacy and moral norms of the past. Despite the occasional celebratory declarations about Ancient Greece, Renaissance humanism, and the Enlightenment, the EU intelligentsia felt uneasy with affirming and genuinely embracing the values that these historical moments stood for. In particular, it was unable to acknowledge the historical contribution of Christianity to European civilization for fear that it would disturb the secular consensus of post-Second World War Europe. Unlike pre-Second World War Secular Liberal and Socialist thought, which recognized Christianity's enormous contribution to European civilization, the intellectual partisans surrounding the EU were too insecure to acknowledge what was an incontrovertible historical fact.[71]

This mood of cultural insecurity was exposed during the debate on the preamble to the EU's proposed Constitution in 2004. Throughout this debate, the West European media tended to treat Christianity as a 'controversial question'. Seven of the member states led by Italy urged the EU to recognize a 'historical truth' and include an explicit reference to the 'Christian roots of Europe' in its proposed Constitution. However, the majority opinion in the EU took the view that such a course of action would exclude Muslims and Jews and therefore it would be wrong to have references to the role of religion. The European Parliament went so far as to reject a proposal from Christian Democrat MEPs to include a reference to the continent's 'Judaeo-Christian roots'.[72] Even the reference to God was considered to be too controversial by many European parliamentarians. In the end, the preamble to the draft Constitution adopted the tactic of using the words 'spiritual', 'religious' and 'humanistic' to describe Europe's cultural heritage. However, MEPs were just about brave enough to refer to traditions in Europe 'nourished by the Greek and Roman civilizations'.[73]

The debate on the preamble of the draft European Constitution is often presented as a conflict between modern secular political thought and old-fashioned religious dogma. But despite the historical tension between temporal and religious authority, the secular *per se* is not necessarily hostile or fearful of religion. Historically, liberalism treats religion as a private matter and not as an outlook that must be abolished from the historical memory. The reluctance even to acknowledge the historical role and contribution of religion to the evolution of humanity is a relatively recent development that is bound with the current phase of the Culture War against traditional values.

No doubt differences on the subject of religion played a significant role in the debate on the EU's Constitution. But the fundamental issue at stake was on the question of whether or not the legacy of the past could provide a source of moral guidance for human action in the twenty-first century. From the standpoint of Year Zero history, the issue is not simply that of religion but also the traditions and values of the past. The imperative driving the transnational and cosmopolitan imagination is to distance society from any form of moral language that is rooted in the past.

Moral norms that are drawn on a sense of historical continuity are rejected precisely because they negate the project of promoting policy-led values that are manufactured through process and rule-making. Adopting a clear and unequivocal stand against values that have emerged organically on the basis of historical experience is often motivated by the realization that administratively-constructed norms lack the moral depth to compete with those that are deeply embedded in people's memory. Administratively produced values crafted through the efforts of committees of experts and policymakers lack an organic relationship to a system of belief and shared experience. Such values are inherently unstable because they constantly invite questioning and scepticism. On their own, administratively created rules and procedures lack the moral resources to motivate and give meaning to human life, and the major questions about the meaning of existence are left unresolved.

It is relatively simple for an institution like the EU to reject historically derived moral norms. However, it is much more difficult to invent values that are credible if they have little organic relationship to the past. The solution adopted by the EU was to make a virtue of the decoupling of its outlook from the past and opt for an approach that emphasized difference and unconnected fragments of its kaleidescoping account. Typically its values statement upholds explicitly relativistic conceptions like difference, diversity, and multiculturalism. It focuses on people's attitudes to others rather than on people's values as such. It evades having to engage with the question of making a moral judgment by adopting non-judgmentalism as one of its principal virtues. In the absence of having any actual moral values of its own that it upholds unconditionally, cosmopolitan thought prefers to restrain those who take their own values seriously. That is why in some Western European societies like Britain there are calls to tone down the celebration of Christmas and render religious symbols invisible in public life. In numerous cases, UK employers have banned Christmas decorations from their offices because they do not want to offend other faiths.[74]

It is not surprising that critics of Hungary have seized on the inclusion of references to God and Christianity in the preamble to this nation's Fundamental Law. Whereas the preamble to the draft EU's Constitution sought to distance itself from a Christian historical legacy, the Hungarian Constitution explicitly sought to reconnect its national identity with the past. This difference in approach to the salience of historical conti-nuity is founded upon the contrasting memory politics of those seeking to preserve a sense of nationhood as opposed to those cultivating a cosmopolitan identity.

It is worth noting that for cosmopolitan EU-philes, constitutional references to God and Christianity represent something of a cultural crime. In his call on the EU to intervene to safeguard democracy in Hungary, Jan-Werner Müller cited a state-ment made by Orbán to the effect that the real source of difference between himself and his West European Leftist opponents was that they 'did not like his advocacy of national pride, Christianity and family values'.[75] Müller found this statement offen-sive because he felt that it wrongly attributed the issues at stake to a *Kulturkampf* rather than to Hungary's violation of the EU's institutional norms and practices. Yet as the current controversy on the status of national sovereignty throughout Europe indicates, a Culture War is in full swing – and it is fought by advocates of Year Zero history no less fiercely than its opponents. The memory wars and the cultural con-flicts with which they are aligned will continue at least until Europe begins to take its history more seriously.

Sociological reflections on the memorialization of the Holocaust

After being neglected by Western historical memory in the 1950s and the 1960s, the Holocaust has emerged as a powerful symbol of human barbarism. As we noted previously in our discussion of the EU's adoption of the Holocaust as its defining value, it has also become thoroughly politicized. The Holocaust has been torn from its tragic historical context and transformed into a generic metaphor of evil. Consequently, the remembrance of the Holocaust often has little to do with a genuine act of grieving or remembering, instead, it works as an official ritual that allows sanctimonious politicians and public figures to put their superior moral virtues on public display.

The belated transformation of the Holocaust into a transcendental sacred value in Western Europe was not so much an act of sincere atonement but an attempt to come to terms with the moral malaise afflicting society. The absence of moral clarity, which has led to so much conflict over values has created a demand for symbols and rituals that confer a measure of coherence on the social order. In a world where society finds it difficult to differentiate clearly between right and wrong, it is important that some kind of line is drawn between acceptable and unacceptable behaviour. Without a moral grammar to express ideas about right and wrong, ethical guidance often has a forced and artificial character. For institutions like the EU, the sacralization of the Holocaust has served as an important resource for supporting its moral authority.

The sacralization of the Holocaust has also provided society with a powerful taboo. Not being against the Holocaust is probably the most ritualized and institutionalized taboo operating in Western societies. In 14 countries, Holocaust denial is a crime that, in some cases, carries a prison term of up to ten years. Preaching about the horrors of the Holocaust helps society avoid working out its own moral view of the world. Its transformation into a universal symbol of evil has helped promote a simplistic moral formula: to be against it is good, and to be for it is evil.

The Holocaust has become one of the most overused metaphors for evil in contemporary times. Animal rights activists in Canada refer to a Holocaust of seals; anti-abortion campaigners in the United States have denounced the Holocaust of foetuses; in Australia there is talk about the Holocaust against Aborigines. Then there is the African American Holocaust, the Serbian Holocaust, the Bosnian Holocaust, and the Rwandan Holocaust. The label 'Holocaust' can be appropriated to attack just about any target, from the erosion of biodiversity to a loss of jobs. Moral entrepreneurs constantly embrace the Holocaust to lend legitimacy to their enterprise. They also insist that anyone who questions their version of events should be treated in a manner that is similar to those who deny the real Holocaust. The expansion of the usage of the Holocaust metaphor has the unintended consequence of gradually diminishing its moral impact.

The demand that we 'learn the lessons of the Holocaust' has become a regular refrain that is adopted to promote a bewildering variety of causes. Frequently, warnings about a particular problem or threat are concluded with the assertion of 'it is just like the Holocaust', 'just like the Nazis', or 'it may lead to a Holocaust'. Such statements offer a claim for moral authority and can be deployed in the most unlikely of circumstances. When the Australian feminist Germaine Greer walked out of the Celebrity Big Brother House in January 2005, she attacked her housemates for refusing to support her defiant stand against the "fascist" bullying of Big Brother.

'Persecution is what happens, holocausts are what happens when good people do nothing', she lectured the public.[76]

Greer's throwaway remarks exemplify a widespread tendency to instrumentalize the sense of sincere guilt and horror that images of the Holocaust can provoke. Unfortunately, this rhetorical strategy often leads to the cynical manoeuvre of guilt-tripping. Within Europe, countries are often judged on whether or not they make the mandatory gestures of remembrance. Sometimes they are criticized for not devoting sufficient resources to the teaching of 'the lessons of the Holocaust'. For example, two educators, Swaan van Iterson & Maja Nenadović, have indicted Hungarian schools for not facing up to the history of the Second World War. They argue that the lack of resources devoted to this task is not unconnected to presence of extremism and anti-Semitism in Hungarian society,[77] and they write that the 'Hungarian educational system's failure to deal adequately with Hungary's World War II history and the country's role in the Holocaust, has to be considered in evaluating the causes of present-day anti-Semitism, Romaphobia, and xenophobia in Hungary'.[78]

Van Iterson and Nenadović, are not simply interested in the provision of quality Holocaust education – they are relying on the moral authority of the Holocaust to substantiate their argument against the teaching of Hungarian national history itself. They claim that:

> History lessons in Hungary regularly seem to convey a pervasive sense of national victimhood, loss, betrayal, and injustice. Such lessons have been criticized for paying too much attention to ancient and medieval history at the expense of twentieth-century history, its legacy and impact on the current events.[79]

Their criticism of 'paying too much attention' to ancient and medieval history constitutes an argument against a curriculum that takes seriously the question of historical continuity. Their usage of the phrase 'at the expense of twentieth history' exposes an approach that assumes that all the events of the past must be subordinated to the memory of the Holocaust.

There is no doubt that Hungary, like many other societies, remains blighted by the curse of anti-Semitism. But the constant exhortation by Western moral entrepreneurs to 'remember the Holocaust' has, if anything, provoked cynicism. In a fascinating essay, Agnes Gagyi offers an incisive account of the way that the issue of anti-Semitism was turned into a political football and used by different parties for contrasting objectives. She cites the example of the anti-Semitic MDF politician, István Csurka, who sought to connect Western support for Hungarian politicians of Jewish origins in the Liberal Party with his argument that this coalition represented a conspiracy against the nation.[80] In response, 'the Socialist-Liberal block stigmatized any mentioning of international dependence or economic plight connected to Hungary's capitalist integration as anti-Semitic "Csurkism"'.[81] In this way, any serious criticism of the deleterious economic impact of the terms on which post-regime change Hungary was integrated into the global markets could be criticized as anti-Semitic.

In effect, the charge of anti-Semitism was turned into a weapon to discredit nationalist politics. Gagyi observed that,

> The polarization of post-socialist Hungarian elites resulted in two, mutually reinforcing constellations of symbolic bridging between elite blocks and their constituencies. Conservatives claimed to defend 'national' interest against the coalition of old socialist power and foreign capital, invoking sentiments of national identity to bridge the gap between the interests of national capital and proletarianized groups. The coalition of Socialists and Liberals relied heavily on Conservatives' definition of 'national interest', and built its legitimacy on defending democracy from 'national interest' as an anti-Semitic, nationalist, populist claim.[82]

One of the lamentable consequences of this debate was the growing practice of treating nationalism, populism, and anti-Semitism as mutually harmonious concepts. This interpretation – particularly as it related to Hungary – was readily assimilated by partisans of the EU, who then began to promote the claim that Hungary is a uniquely anti-Semitic society. Their constant focus on Hungarian anti-Semitism not only encouraged a mood of Holocaust fatigue, but it also triggered resentment of those who promoted this message.

Back in January 2006, I warned in an article in *The Daily Telegraph* that the transformation of the Holocaust into a political symbol and its constant usage threatened to deprive it of its important moral meaning.[83] Worse still, the more that the terrible experience of the Nazi era has become institutionalized through Holocaust days, Holocaust memorials and museums, Holocaust curricula, and Holocaust films, the more it has become a focus of competitive claims-making.

I noted that instead of serving as a focus of unity, Holocaust Day merely encourages different groups to develop an inflated sense of past suffering and to demand public recognition for it. It encourages different cultural groups to represent themselves as victims of historical injustices. Such a response is not surprising, since it is difficult for a single experience of barbaric violence to serve as a universal symbol of suffering. It is one thing to recognize the scale of destruction and the unique dimension of the Holocaust. It is quite another to turn it into a moral tale that can inspire all people at all times.

If Holocaust Day were just another meaningless ritual, there would be little reason for concern. But such initiatives actually help create an environment that encourages scepticism about what actually happened during the Nazi era. False morality always incites the response of cynicism, and Holocaust-mongering is no exception. In 2004, a poll conducted in nine European countries by the Ipsos MORI market research organization indicated that 35 percent of those interviewed stated that Jews should stop playing the role of Holocaust victims. Although the Western media usually castigates East European societies – particularly Hungary – for tolerating anti-Semitism, it is worth noting that none of these nine countries were behind the old Iron Curtain. They are Italy, France, Belgium, Spain, Austria, the Netherlands, Luxembourg, Germany, and Britain.[84]

At present, this mood of scepticism is still unformed. But it is only a matter of time before the obsessive institutionalization of the cult of the Holocaust will create a situation where scepticism will invite disbelief.

The concerns that I raised in January 2006 have become far more relevant to the situation today. Scepticism, and even the denial, of the Holocaust has grown significantly – and in parallel with the expansion of public initiatives designed to memorialize it. A report circulated in January 2017 citing Dr Nicholas Terry, a history lecturer at Exeter University, estimates that there are now thousands of 'low-commitment' Holocaust deniers online.[85] In December 2016, the top hit on Google in response to a search for the question 'Did the Holocaust happen?' was a link that claimed that the murder of six million Jews was a hoax.[86]

It is inconceivable that back in the 1950s, 1960s, or 1970s – before the public sacralization of Holocaust memory took off – there would have been such an interest in conspiracy theories that suggested that this act of genocide was a hoax. The experience of recent decades suggests that those who are interested in a genuine memorialization of the Holocaust need to take their distance from the current practice of treating it as a memory to which all others must be subordinated.

Notes

1 www.theguardian.com/football/2012/feb/22/david-cameron-government-racism-football.
2 Cited in *The Independent;* 28 April 1990.
3 Mudde, C. (2016) 'Can We Stop the Politics of Nostalgia That Have Dominated 2016', 15 December 2016, http://europe.newsweek.com/1950s-1930s-racism-us-europe-nostalgia-cas-mudde-531546?rm=eu.
4 Meier (2005) p. 17.
5 Meier (2005) p. 17.
6 See Ónody-Mo, D. (2016) 'Why Are Statues in Hungary So Controversial?', 18 May 2016, www.getthetrollsout.org/what-we-do/articles/item/74-why-are-statues-in-hungary-so-controversial.html.
7 Theiler (2005).
8 Cited in Kaiser (2015).
9 Settele (2015) p. 405.
10 Calligaro (2015) p. 332.
11 'Consolidating New democracies' by Hannes Swoboda and Jan Marius Wiersma, Booklet published by Socialist group in 2008, www.socialistsanddemocrats.eu../sites/default/files/2631_EN_democracy-populism_web_1.pdf.
12 Larat (2005) pp. 278–279.
13 Della Sala (2010) pp. 1, 3.
14 Mälksoo (2009) p. 357.
15 Della Sala (2016) p. 524.
16 Behr (2007) p. 250.
17 His speech is available on Orbán Viktor 2007. októberi 1-i beszéde a Lakiteleki Találkozó 20. Évfordulóján, *2007. október 1.* http://2007-2010.orbanviktor.hu/beszedek_list.php?item=27.

18 Habermas (1988) p. 5.
19 See Konrad (1984) p. 185.
20 Konrad (1984) p. 70.
21 Szabó (1991) p. 177.
22 See Kokut (2012) Chapter 4.
23 Fowler (2004)
24 Martín-Arroyo (2014) p. 45.
25 Berger (2007) pp. 65–66.
26 Larat (2005) p. 273.
27 Larat (2005) p. 287.
28 'Citizenship Education Facing Nationalism and Populism in Europe Strategies – Competencies – Practices East-West concepts of nationalism in light of EU integration', Fabrice Larat, National School of Administration (Strasbourg) Sofia, Bulgaria, November 6–8, 2008, www.nece.eu.
29 Shore (1999) p. 31.
30 Cited in Klinke (2014) p. 575.
31 Calliagro is cited in Klinke (2014) p. 574.
32 Auer (2010) p. 1176.
33 See Kaiser (2015) p. 364.
34 See Kaiser (2015) p. 368.
35 'Citizenship Education Facing Nationalism and Populism in Europe Strategies – Competencies – Practices East-West concepts of nationalism in light of EU integration', Paper given by Fabrice Larat, National School of Administration (Strasbourg) Sofia, Bulgaria, November 6–8, 2008, www.nece.eu.
36 Mikulova (2013) p. 169.
37 Larat, F. 'The Role of the Acquis Historique Communautaire in EU-Governance', www.mzes.uni-mannheim.de/d7/en/publications/presentation/paper-the-role-of-the-acquis-historique-communautaire-in-eu-governance.
38 Closa (2011) p. 9.
39 www.hansardsociety.org.uk/blogs/citizenship_education/archive/2011/05/09/3032.aspx.
40 www.hansardsociety.org.uk/blogs/citizenship_education/archive/2011/05/09/3032.aspx. p. 3.
41 See for example the website of the European Commission 'Education and Training' – http://ec.europa.eu/education/comenius/doc859_en.htm
42 Della Sala (2016) p. 525.
43 Della Sala (2016) p. 525.
44 Cvijic & Zucca (2004) p. 739.
45 Littoz-Monnet, A. (2013) 'Explaining Policy Conflict across Institutional Venues: European Union-Level Struggles over the Memory of the Holocaust', Journal of *Common Market Studies, vol.* 51, no.3 (2013): p.13.
46 Littoz-Monnet (2013) p. 1.
47 Karlsson (2010) p. 40.
48 Müller (2007) p. 101.
49 Cited in Karlsson (210) p. 41.
50 Littoz-Monnet (2013) p. 6.
51 Müller (2007) p. 107.
52 Cited in Karlsson (210) p. 41.
53 Della Sala (2016)
54 Laure Neumayer (2015) p. 346.
55 Littoz-Monnet (2013) p. 2.
56 Littoz-Monnet (2013) p. 2.
57 Neumayer (2015) p. 344.
58 Neumayer (2015) p. 344.
59 Mälksoo (2009)

60 Neumayer (2015) p. 349.
61 Cited in Neumayer (2015) p. 349.
62 Cited in Neumayer (2015) p. 353.
63 Mälksoo (2009) p. 356.
64 Littoz-Monnet (2013) p. 6.
65 Neumayer (2015) p. 346.
66 Rousso (2016) p. 73.
67 Orban's speech is cited on www.ce-review.org/00/8/essay8.html#b2.
68 Lánczi, A. (2002) 'Konzervatív kiáltvány', *Élet és Irodalom*, vol. 46, 15 November 2002.
69 Kaiser (2015) pp. 374–375.
70 Kaiser (2015) pp. 374–375.
71 For a classical socialist assessment of Christianity see Kautsy, K. (1925) *Foundations of Christianity: A Study in Christian Origins*, George Allen & Unwin: London, First published in German in 1908.
72 See Ian Black, I. 'Christianity Bedevils Talks on EU Treaty', *The Guardian*, 25 May 2004, www.theguardian.com/world/2004/may/25/eu.religion.
73 For an account of this debate see www.wnd.com/2003/05/19030/#WqG0MjKH4hW wkoz5.99.
74 See 'Christmas Ban "For Fear of Offence"', *Yorkshire Post*, 6 December 2006.
75 Müller, J.-W. (2013) *Safeguarding Democracy Inside the EU Brussels and the Future of Liberal Order*, Transatlantic Academy Paper Series, p.19, http://www.transatlanticacademy.org/publications/safeguarding-democracy-inside-eu-brussels-and-future-liberal-order.
76 www.theguardian.com/media/2005/jan/12/bigbrother.broadcasting.
77 van Iterson & Nenadović (2013) pp. 93–102.
78 van Iterson & Nenadović (2013) p. 94.
79 van Iterson & Nenadović (2013) p. 97.
80 Gagyi (2016) p. 356.
81 Gagyi (2016) p. 356.
82 Gagyi (2016) p. 356.
83 Furedi, F. (2006) 'The Holocaust Is Not For Sale', *The Daily Telegraph*, 26 January 2006.
84 www.haaretz.com/35-of-europeans-say-jews-should-stop-playing-the-victim-1.112128.
85 www.theguardian.com/world/2017/jan/22/online-conspiracy-theories-feed-holocaust-denial.
86 https://mic.com/articles/165038/did-the-holocaust-happen-google-s-top-search-results-still-say-it-s-a-hoax#.9ShJauPvH.

5

ANTI-POPULISM AND THE CRISIS OF VALUATION

One of the curious consequences of the memory wars is that the line between the past and the present has become blurred and confused. It is difficult to pick up a newspaper without encountering references to the Second World War or the Weimar Republic. Arguments over the alleged problem of populism or Euroscepticism inevitably lead to asides about the imminent danger of fascism – indeed, fascism has become an all-purpose epithet that can be hurled at any target of a disagreement. Hungary, in particular, has become the object of accusation that it has become either a fascist nation or is on the road to becoming a fascist dictatorship. Since the election of Donald Trump to the American Presidency, the 'f word' has also migrated across the Atlantic. The cultural script of anti-populism warns that a return to the fascist era is the inexorable outcome of populist politics.

The tendency to interpret twenty-first-century issues directly through the memory of the tragic events of the 1930s and 1940s is motivated, in part, by a fear about returning to the bad old days and in part by a sublimated expression of anxiety about the contemporary moral order. It is the uncertainty about the resilience of the moral order that has led a significant section of the Western political and cultural establishment to periodically express its angst about the dangers of a 'return of nationalism' or, worse still, of some type of totalitarian movement. This sentiment remains integral to the outlook of many of the liberal Eastern European dissidents who achieved a prominent role during the transition to the post-Soviet era. Many of these intellectual dissidents, who had developed a close association with their Western co-thinkers, came to adopt the conviction that the revitalization of national sentiment in post-Soviet societies was the greatest threat to the establishment of democracy in their countries.

In the 1980s and 1990s, Western NGOs and international institutions collaborated with East European liberal intellectuals and politicians to educate post-communist societies about the pitfalls of nationalism and the virtues of a non-national, civic values based society. These initiatives were inspired by the concern that former members of the Warsaw Pact were historically disposed towards the embrace of highly volatile and irrational forms of ethnic nationalism. Curing East Europe from its proclivity to adopt immoderate national sentiments was one of the main themes at a three-day conference of the Soros-MTA Foundation in Krakow in September 1991. This subject was the focus of Hungarian émigré Péter Kende's speech, 'Return to Tradition . . . What Tradition?', in Kraków:

> One has to relativize the so-called national traditions which originate more in rhetoric and pious wishes than the real state of collective conscience. Nothing is more uncertain, fleeting and ill than this conscience. One has to invest, now that the moment of healing has come, not in the exploration of the past, . . . but in the reconstitution of the national collective on the basis of civic virtues inherent to a democracy: the defense of rights, the toleration of difference and active solidarity (liberté – égalité – fraternité).[1]

For Kende, the 'moment of healing' required a determination to avoid an exploration of the past. His speech articulated a lack of empathy and sensitivity towards the meaning that national tradition and sentiment could have for large sections of society. That is why national traditions were prefaced by the de-legitimizing term 'so-called'. His call to 'relativize' national tradition in effect represented the aspiration to deprive them of meaning.

Kende intuitively feared the durability and power of 'resurgent nationalism'. Yet he could not face up to this challenge, which is why he unwittingly contradicts himself by claiming that this national conscience was 'uncertain' and 'fleeting'. For Kende and his colleagues in Kraków – consistency national sentiment was a disease that required a political cure. Kende himself appeared to be drawn towards Habermas' idea of constitutional patriotism. However, the very attempt to recast patriotism into a neutral, non-national affiliation to legally binding rules only highlighted his isolation from the realities of people's lived experience.

At least one person who attended the conference in Kraków understood that in East Europe, national conscience was far from fleeting. Marion Gräfin Dönhoff, editor of *Die Zeit*, wrote after the conference:

> There in Cracow, I realized that nationalism, which we Westerners regard with a lot of skepticism, had been indispensable for the survival of the East Europeans. That was the only way they had been able to fight for their identity and finally achieve freedom.[2]

Dönhoff recognized that the possession of a robust national identity was essential for the achievement of freedom in East Europe. Nevertheless, in line with the mainstream ethos of West European political culture, she concluded that now, 'everything depends on them . . . [East Europeans] . . . returning to a form of normal liberalism'.

In all but name, Kende's exhortation to 'relativize' national traditions represented a call to dispossess history of a sense of continuity, or at least to empty society's memory of most of its national traditions. This response, fuelled by a one-dimensional interpretation of the national as an inherently volatile and dangerous phenomenon, was widely shared by many prominent leftist and liberal Hungarian intellectuals and politicians. Consequently, they adopted a policy of minimizing its significance. They tended to approach outstanding historical issues, such as the legacy of the Treaty of Trianon, as an irritating diversion to be avoided rather than as an opportunity to work out policies that would offer Hungarians a new focus for their national identity. One account of this debate noted that since 1989, 'the right wing has kept the Trianon trauma in the agenda as a source of nationalism while the left has swept the problem under the carpet'. The Hungarian émigré journalist Paul Lendvai wrote that 'as a consequence of the populist, increasingly aggressive rhetoric of the right and the passivity of the left, the rightwing interpretation of Trianon has prevailed among the adult population in the last decade'.[3]

What Lendvai characterized as the 'passivity' of the left on the issue of Trianon – that is, a failure to address the national question – was the outcome of an acute sense of anxiety having to engage with the public's national sensibilities. On matters such as Trianon, it preferred historical amnesia to remembrance, and regarded national consciousness as a volatile, inherently dangerous force that needed to be prevented from influencing public life.

To a significant extent, the hostility towards the sense of nationhood that characterized the outlook of the EU oligarchy was refracted through Hungarian domestic politics. In the aftermath of regime change, those in leftist and liberal political circles sought to consolidate their authority by developing a close special relationship with the West. They used their informal alliance with Western institutions and their representatives to promote the claim that they were best placed to promote the interest of Hungary in a globalized world. This orientation towards external political actors further distanced this layer of Hungarian society from national realities. The anti-nationalist political culture of the informal alliance between the EU leadership and the Hungarian liberal left provoked a reaction from conservative nationalists, who sometimes perceived Western institutions as the allies of their political opponents. The reliance of the Hungarian liberal left on its connections with Western transnational institutions, NGOs, and the EU oligarchy had the cumulative effect of weakening its capacity to engage with the problems facing the people of Hungary. These factors 'created an environment which has undermined support for the cosmopolitan ideals of Hungary's left-liberal political elites,' concedes a bitter critic of the Orbán Government.[4]

Matters were made worse by the proclivity of anti-Fidesz political actors to call on the EU and Western governments to fight its domestic battles in Hungary. The self-defined left has adopted the practice of writing open letters and articles imploring Western political actors to put pressure on the Hungarian government to put right the wrongs it had committed. In placing faith on its transnational Western co-thinkers, rather than attempting to appeal to and mobilize Hungarian public opinion, it reinforces its isolation from society.

The hostility directed against Hungarian national sensibilities by the left/liberal bloc echoed the EU's proclivity to promote diversity and minority rights as a counterpoint to the authority of the nation. From their standpoint, minority rights were *de facto* logically prior and morally superior to the principle of nationality. Their affirmation of identity politics, paralleled by their devaluation of national sentiment, constituted the pivotal point in an undeclared Culture War. In effect minority rights served as a medium through which nationalist claims could be restrained and put in its place. As Agnes Gagyi argued, as against the upholding of 'the symbolic value of the nation' by conservatives, their opponents offered a version of solidarity that was directed at the defence of groups 'typically referred as minorities (Roma, Jews, women, LGBTQ)'. Gagyi wrote:

> This practice split social grievances into illegitimate nationalist claims, and legitimate minority claims. The conservative bloc could easily rely on that split in its own symbolic compensation techniques, to argue that the nation is under attack by alien interests both from above and below. One stinging implication of that argument was that the aid Liberals, the Soros Foundation, and their Western partners offer to the Roma contributes to the demographic threat they represent to Hungarians. That argument, on its turn, worked to solidify democratic antipopulists' claim to defend democracy and minorities from Hungarians' racism.[5]

Although Gagyi is not a friend of the conservative bloc, she recognized that the purpose of the importation of EU style identity politics into Hungary was to de-legitimate nationalist politics.

One of the unfortunate consequences of the tactic of attempting to devalue nationalist claims by elevating those of minorities to a pre-eminent status was to encourage an unresolvable conflict of interest between the two. It set in motion a dynamic whereby both sides would see their claims as directly antithetical to one another.

The meaning of anti-populism

The constant allusions to 'it's just like the 1930s', together with expressions of anxiety about resurgent nationalism, can be interpreted as a form of psychological displacement of the concern about people's ability to behave as responsible citizens. Since the 1930s, liberal-democratic theory has been unsettled by the realization that, at least in part, Hitler's rise to power was based on his electoral success. The relative success of the Nazi Party in using elections to its advantage was interpreted as a warning about the unreliability of the electorate. Many opponents of Nazism adopted a mistrustful stance regarding the workings of popular democracy. They could no longer take for granted the competence and reliability of citizens to act responsibly.

The German social psychologist Erich Fromm voiced his pessimistic diagnosis of the events of the 1930s in the following terms: 'we have been compelled to recognize that millions in Germany were as eager to surrender their freedom as their fathers were to fight for it'.[6] The political philosopher and social reformer John Dewey tended to regard the psychological attitudes of the masses as a threat to democracy in the United States. 'The serious threat to our democracy,' he asserted, 'is not the existence of foreign totalitarian states', but the 'existence within our personal attitudes and within our own institutions of conditions which have given a victory to external authority, discipline, uniformity and dependence upon The Leader'.[7]

By the mid-1930s, democracy itself was frequently held responsible for unleashing the destructive and irrational powers sweeping the world. In his 1933 essay 'The Democratization of Culture', the Hungarian-born sociologist Károly Mannheim asserted that it was democracy itself that created the terrain for the flourishing of totalitarian movements:

> Dictatorships can arise only in democracies; they are made possible by the greater fluidity introduced into political life by democracy. Dictatorship is not the antithesis of democracy; it represents one of the possible ways in which a democratic society may try to solve its problems.[8]

In the decades that followed, the scepticism of liberal commentators towards democracy hardened. In particular, apprehensions about the capacity of the *demos* to resist the totalitarian temptation of nationalism were frequently voiced.

It is in the context of this long-standing apprehension about the sway of xenophobic nationalism over the public imagination that the cosmopolitan ideology of the EU needs to be situated. Its rigid and unyielding anti-populist stance communicates both a fear of, and a disdain for, the people. Its defensive attitude towards the *demos* has if anything become far more entrenched since the Eurozone crisis of 2008. Orbán's assessment of the EU's anti-populism places it in its proper historical context. Orbán argued, in 2002, that in the post-Second World War era Western leaders:

> feared not communism or fascism any more, but the masses, especially the politically active masses. Because of the fact that fascism won power democratically, today's Western European elite thinks that one should be cautious with the people, because the decisions of the people can cause big difficulties. So, democracy is regarded by them to be important but it is still better if power is not exercised by the people. This is how one can summarise the attitude of contemporary Western-European elite towards the people, towards its own people.[9]

As we discuss later, the Western European political class, particularly the leadership of the EU, regards popular democracy with ambivalence. Its strong strand of anti-populism is, at least in part, stirred by an apprehension about the reliability of national electorates. That is why Habermas can so casually write off national electorates as 'the preserve of right-wing nationalism' and condemn them as 'the caricature of national macrosubjects shutting themselves off from each other'.[10] His reaction and those of his fellow EU-philes is an outcome of its recognition that when it comes to a political debate with nationalist parties, they struggle to win the hearts and minds of the public. They find it easier to blame the ignorance and prejudices of the people than acknowledge the difficulty they have in elaborating a compelling normative foundation for their authority.

The upshot of this hesitant ambivalence towards the people is that despite an avowal to the principles of liberal democracy, many Western cosmopolitan commentators and their Hungarian allies regard democracy as a mixed blessing that needs to be exercised with clinical care. Kim Lane Scheppele, one of the most hostile critics of Hungarian conservative nationalist politics, personifies the suspicion that anti-majoritarian commentators display towards popular sovereignty. This sociology professor from Princeton University constantly alerts Western policymakers and the public about Hungary's slide towards an authoritarian society. Yet she is less than enamoured by the exercise of freedom through the workings of representative democracy.

Scheppele, like many supporters of the EU's style of technocratic governance, is an enthusiastic supporter of judicial activism and the practice of endowing the courts with great political power and authority. She regarded the Hungarian Constitutional Court, which was the outcome of the roundtable negotiations that led to regime change, with great affection. Her preferences are clearly articulated in the title of her essay, 'Democracy By Judiciary (Or Why The Courts Can Sometimes Be More Democratic Than Parliaments)'.[11] Scheppele saw the newly established Hungarian Constitutional Court as a positive alternative to politicians squabbling in Parliament. From her standpoint, the messy business of electoral politics needed to be tamed, and ultimately controlled, by a powerful court run by a small group of unelected judges.

Like the Constitutional Court established in West Germany after the Second World War, the aim of its Hungarian equivalent was to insulate the political system from popular pressure. As László Sólyom, president of the Constitutional Court from 1990 to 1998 and President of Hungary from 2005 to 2010, explained:

> The new constitutional courts were created out of a deep mistrust for the majoritarian institutions, which had been misused and corrupted in the Fascist and Communist regimes. In this given historical setting, the constitutional courts believed they represented the essence of the democratic change, and enjoyed 'revolutionary legitimacy'. Little wonder if some constitutional courts have been inclined to replace the motto 'we the people' with 'we the court'.[12]

To his credit, Sólyom acknowledged the fact that an unelected group of judges could, in all but name, override the influence of the people and their parliamentary representatives. The ascendancy of such a powerful judicial institution was linked to the transition deal forged by the Westernized Hungarian elites and their EU negotiating partners.[13] For many EU technocrats, the establishment of a powerful counter-majoritarian institution like the Constitutional Court offered a guarantee that Hungary would behave in accordance with their political ethos.

When the Constitutional Court was established in 1989, there was very little disquiet raised about the formidable powers that this institution possessed. At the time, one of the few to raise concern about this development was the Hungarian legal scholar Béla Pokol, who argued that the power awarded to the Hungarian Constitutional Court was far greater than anywhere else in Europe. He explained that:

> In Hungary, a Constitutional Court keeps in check the parliamentary major-ity and the government, and this Constitutional Court is relatively perhaps more powerful than any other judiciary body anywhere in the world, and our ombudsman further widen, as watchdogs of the constitutional rights, the sphere of checks and balances vis-à-vis government.[14]

In effect, in its early phase, the Hungarian Constitutional Court possessed powers that are usually associated with the executive. As Scheppele explained:

> In creating the Constitutional Court, the Roundtable had effectively created a new governmental system that was not presidentialism or parliamentarian-ism (the usual two choices), but instead a 'courtocracy'. Through the early 1990s, the Constitutional Court was for all intents and purposes running the country. Or at least the Court had as much power in the Hungarian system as the President has in France or the Parliament in the UK.[15]

Scheppele assertion that this arrangement was more democratic than parliamentary democracy serves as testimony of the anti-populist disdain for both popular and parliamentary sovereignty. Instead of the people being the authors of their law, they become its submissive recipients in Scheppele ideal scenario.

One reason for the high regard that Scheppele had towards the newly established Constitutional Court was that this institution promised to enforce the outlook of the EU's political culture in Hungarian society. She was delighted that the Court 'frankly adopted the precedents of other European constitutional courts in deciding what the Hungarian Constitution meant', and remarked that:

> This has led to a dominant 'transnational constitutionalism' in which the prin-ciples of the Hungarian constitutional order are assessed against the backdrop of internationally agreed-upon ideas of what a constitutional, rule-of-law democratic republic should be. Soviet-era laws were selectively struck down as unconstitutional only if, upon review, they were found to violate some specific aspect of the new, liberal, democratic Constitution.[16]

Her preference for transnational constitutionalism even extended to a willingness 'selectively' to perpetuate the authority of some 'Soviet-era laws'.

Aside from the dubious democratic credentials of an omnipotent Constitutional Court, the aim of its transnational constitutionalism was to dispossess, or at least restrain, the kind of law-making that is based on the exercise of national sovereignty. Scheppele response to subsequent measures taken to develop a more Hungarian version of constitutional law exemplifies an intemperate sense of intolerance and insensitivity to the project. Her denunciation of Hungarian conservative jurisprudence and its attempt to endow the Crown of Saint Stephen with constitutional significance evoked the spectre of an imminent return of the dark forces of fascism. She warned, back in 2000:

> Since much of this discourse emphasizes the ethnic purity and territorial ambitions of the ideal Hungarian state, it is but a short step from there to the justification of fascist politics. That is what defenders of transnational constitutionalism have to fear from the new Hungarian constitutional conservatism. The crown stands, simply enough, for much of what is dangerous in contemporary Hungary.[17]

Scheppele could have provided a reasoned argument based on liberal constitutional principles against her conservative opponents. But like many of her co-thinkers, she opted for the simplistic scare tactic of warning, that it is but a 'short step there to the justification of fascist politics'. What is particularly tendentious about the stance adopted by Scheppele and many other critics of 'authoritarian' politics in Hungary is that they are very selective about which kind of authoritarianism they do not like. They have little objection to authoritarianism as such – so long as it is exercised by a small group of transnationally educated, unelected judges.

Since the enactment of the Fundamental Law in January 2012, the power of the Hungarian Constitutional Court has significantly diminished. The loss of authority of the Constitutional Court has not been welcomed by the EU technocracy and international advocates of transnational constitutionalism and judicial activism, and it is frequently cited by international critics of the Fidesz government as proof of its violation of liberal standards of democracy. However, what these critics fail to acknowledge is that this institution was established in its original form precisely to restrain the exercise of democracy and parliamentary democracy.

Although Jan-Werner Müller has called on the EU to intervene in Hungarian domestic affairs in order to 'safeguard' democracy, he at least recognized that the founding of constitutional courts have little to do with the objective of expanding democracy. He wrote that in post-war Western Europe, constitutional courts were adopted in order to insulate the institutions of the state from pressure from below:

> The architects of the post-war West European order viewed the ideal of popular sovereignty with a great deal of distrust. After all, how could one trust peoples who had brought fascists to power or extensively collaborated with fascist occupiers? Less obviously, elites also had deep reservations about the idea of parliamentary sovereignty.[18]

Not trusting people to do the right thing is at the core of transnational constitutionalism. As far as the EU was concerned, when it comes to not trusting people, Hungarians and East Europeans are in a class of their own. Writing in this vein, Müller alludes to the fact that the imperative of constraining democracy through a Constitutional Court does not necessarily apply to all countries. He cites the example of Britain 'where de facto constraints on – in theory unlimited – parliamentary sovereignty have had a more informal character'. Apparently unlike in the more politically backwards societies of East Europe, people in Britain 'are more likely to trust themselves, instead of empowering unelected institutions'.[19]

Distrust of the people and parliamentary sovereignty is reinforced by the concern that, on its own, liberal democracy lacks the normative foundation to inspire the loyalty and affection of ordinary citizens. The political culture of the EU and of transnational legal theory avoids the need to engage with the electorate and to convince citizens to adopt views that are generally unpopular in wider society. It relies on the authority of transnational or international institutions to avoid having to win the argument on contentious issues – especially those with a moral dimension, such as capital punishment. Anthony Barnett, despite being an editor of a publication titled *openDemocracy*, illustrates this instinct to constrain the exercise of the popular will. He stated that he is staunchly against 'the UK parliament taking a decision on the death penalty', claiming to be reassured that Britain's elected Parliament 'may debate but it cannot in fact introduce the death penalty', because the European Court of Human Rights has 'ruled that the death penalty does in fact contravene the European Convention [on Human Rights]'.[20]

One reason why the West European political establishment is prepared to endow the European Court of Human Rights with a quasi-sacred authority is to ensure that fundamental questions touching on moral norms are taken out of the realm of politics. The outsourcing of moral and political authority to an apparently independent institution like the Court of Human Rights or the Constitutional Court is symptomatic of the difficulty that post-war liberal democracy has in dealing with the realm of values.

The institutionalization of anti-majoritarian practices is accepted as sound practice by partisans of the EU. In addition to depoliticizing decision-making through the use of courts, the supporters of the federalist project in Europe rely on expert and technocratic authority to assume responsibility for policy-making. Andrew Moravcsik, professor in international relations, outlined the justification for this procedure in the following terms:

> The apparently 'counter-majoritarian' tendency of the EU political institutions insulated from direct democratic contestation arises out of factors that themselves have normative integrity, notably efforts to compensate for the ignorance and nonparticipation of citizens, to make terrible commitments to rights enforcement, and to offset the power of special interests.[21]

From this standpoint, the existence of popular sovereignty serves to distort the running of the institutions of the EU, and counter-majoritarian institutions are necessary to tame the people.

The two faces of illiberalism

In recent years, anti-populist political commentators appear to be obsessed with the interrelated topics of the crisis of liberalism and the threat posed by populism to a free and open society. An exemplar of this genre of scaremongering literature was an article published in *Foreign Policy* in July 2016. The short essay, titled 'Liberalism Isn't Working' and written by the American journalist James Traub, conveyed a sense of quiet despair. The target of Traub's polemic was the alleged rise of illiberalism and the peril that it represented to the survival of liberal-democratic values. One of the main targets of his article was Hungary. 'I wonder if the West is sleep-walking towards "illiberal democracy," the ideology championed by Hungary's Viktor Orbán', he asked.[22] Although Traub highlighted Orbán as the leader of his illiberal Rogue's Gallery, he also castigated Poland's Law and Justice Party, Donald Trump, and Turkey's 'increasingly autocratic' Prime Minister Recep Tayyip Erdogan, for endorsing elements of the 'ideology' of illiberal democracy.

Before exploring the meaning of 'illiberal democracy', it is important to note that Traub and his fellow critics of populism often adopt a double standard when it comes to the question of illiberalism. This is particularly the case in the context of the debates surrounding the EU. The EU's partisans frequently imply that any challenge to this body is comparable to the kind of attacks that illiberal forces mounted against democratic institutions in the interwar era. Their criticism is conveyed in a dramatic tone, and it frequently concludes with the illiberal assertion that those who defy the authority of the EU are the enemy of *liberal democracy*. Donald Tusk, the president of the European Council, recently characterized Poland's arguments with the EU as an expression of the 'different values and different strategic aims' to those of liberal democracy. And that is not, apparently, permissible, for: 'whoever attacks the European Union harms America,' and 'whoever undermines the foundations of liberal democracy harms one and the other'.[23] Scepticism towards the EU is no longer regarded as a legitimate standpoint: it is condemned as the ideology of the enemy.

Traub also possesses an unabashedly illiberal elitist view of populism. A week before he went on the offensive against Orbán's illiberalism, Traub penned an article titled 'It's Time for the Elites to Rise Up Against the Ignorant Masses'. Here, he draws out the deep-seated mistrust of the people that has led him and his co-thinkers to react with such bitter hostility against the *demos*. Traub argues that developments such as Britain's vote for Brexit show that the 'political schisms of our time' are not between left and right but 'the sane vs. the mindless angry'.[24] He views the 'ignorant masses' as his moral inferiors who need to be re-educated by the enlightened elites, and comments:

> Did I say 'ignorant'? Yes, I did. It is necessary to say that people are deluded and that the task of leadership is to un-delude them.[25]

The conviction that the people who support the wrong kind of political movements are ignorant and stupid allows Traub to adopt a paternalistic tone that is usually associated with authoritarian elitism. If such a tone of superiority and dehumanizing language was used by his political foes towards people that Traub exempts from the charge of ignorance, it would be condemned as biased, prejudiced, and probably racist.

In the contemporary era, critics of illiberalism often possess attitudes that are very similar to those they attribute to their opponents. However they rarely acknowledge their prejudices and appear blissfully unaware of the way that their bias influences their conduct. They also appear to be unaware of the fact that many of their views have little in common with the tradition of classical liberalism.

Historically, liberalism has been in the forefront of expanding the domain of freedom. As Steven Holmes observed in his important study *The Anatomy of Antiliberalism*, religious toleration and freedom of discussion are two of the 'core practices' of liberalism.[26] Yet in recent times, self-declared liberals have found it difficult to be tolerant of religion and, as we discussed in relation to the debate on the preamble of the proposed EU Constitution, they found it difficult to even recognize the contribution that Christianity made to the European heritage. More importantly, Holmes noted that 'public disagreement could be as a creative force may have been the most novel and radical principle of liberal politics'.[27] Certainly on this point, self-described twenty-first-century liberals have often been found wanting. Throughout the Western world they have been actively engaged in lobbying for laws that regulate and limit the freedom of speech. The new genre of hate laws, which criminalizes the voicing of hate, is the outcome of political campaigning by activists associated with liberal causes.

However, it is within the system of higher education that the paternalistic and authoritarian temper of twenty-first-century liberalism becomes most evident. In universities, liberalism has developed authoritarian tendencies that express themselves in the policing of speech and through social engineering initiatives directed at pressurizing people to alter their views and attitudes.[28] Demonstrators in US universities carrying placards stating 'Free Speech is Hate Speech' illustrate the low regard with which this precious freedom is regarded by sections of the academic community.

That the valuation of free speech is frequently called into question on the campuses of ostensibly liberal universities indicates that almost imperceptibly, the liberal value of tolerance has mutated into the illiberal advocacy of censorship. Critics of the Orbán Government's campaign against the institutional integrity of the Central European University in Budapest rarely raise concerns about the illiberal and censorious climate that prevails on Anglo-American campuses.

The main reason why some Western critics take objection to Viktor Orbán's argument for illiberal democracy is, as we have seen, not because they have a principled objection to illiberalism but because of a fundamental difference in values between their version of illiberalism and that promoted by Orbán. In his July 2014 speech outlining his conception of illiberal democracy, Orbán alluded to the importance that he attached to conservative nationalist values. The outlook that he espoused is conservative, communitarian, nationalist, and Christian. His endorsement of illiberal democracy appears to be a reaction to what he perceived as liberalism's failure to affirm the values that underpin family, community, and national life. His speech stated that the objective of his government was to 'harmonise relationship between the interests and achievement of individuals – that needs to be acknowledged – with interests and achievements of the community, and the nation'. In part, this objective was guided by a reaction to the difficulty that Western polities have in providing their communities with a web of meaning through which their citizens can make sense of their place in the world.

The concept of illiberal democracy outlined in the July 2014 speech is most congruent with the Burkean version of conservative thought. An emphasis on the maintenance of an organic relationship with a community's tradition was a central theme in Edmund Burke's idealization of a contract between generations. As Ferenc Hörcher pointed out, the 'National Avowal', a preamble to the Hungarian Fundamental Law, echoes Burke's well-known analogy of this inter-generational contract. The avowal states:

> Our Fundamental Law shall be the basis of our legal order: it shall be a covenant among Hungarians past, present and future; a living framework which expresses the nation's will and the form in which we want to live.[29]

Unlike the scepticism that liberal philosophy directs towards the values of the past, the Burkean celebration of tradition regards them as providing the moral foundation for political order.

In his speech, Orbán asserted that his commendation of illiberalism was not directed at liberalism as such, but against the project of resting the authority of the state solely on a liberal foundation:

> Hungarian nation is not a simple sum of individuals, but a community that needs to be organized, strengthened and developed, and in this sense, the new state that we are building is an illiberal state, a non-liberal state. It does not deny foundational values of liberalism, as freedom, etc. But it does not make this ideology a central element of state organization, but applies a specific, national, particular approach in its stead.[30]

In other words, this argument asserts that there is more to life then liberalism. What really irritated his Western critics was that this conception of illiberal democracy directly called into question the transnational outlook so central to cosmopolitan ideology. In publicly flaunting his adherence to illiberal democratic values, Orbán communicated the simple message that he was an unashamed nationalist in his cultural outlook and, above all, a Hungarian. This stance was unlikely to endear him to partisans of the anti-nationalist political culture of the EU.

The primacy that Orbán assigned to national interest and the significance that he attached to Christianity was also directly antithetical to the outlook of the EU oligarchy. In addition, its emphasis on supporting and defending the national economy directly challenged the pro-globalization and market liberalization consensus of Brussels.

From the standpoint of cosmopolitan-minded commentators, the most scandalous feature of Orbán's July 2014 speech was that it unashamedly and explicitly advocated values that called into question their moral authority. Whatever the intent that lay behind this speech, many Western policymakers and commentators interpreted it as a provocation, if not a declaration of intent to wage a Culture War against their values. The unapologetic defence of the nation state directly called into question some of the core principles of the EU, such as diversity and multiculturalism. That a leader of an EU member state was prepared to extol the virtues of values that Brussels and other transnational institutions have deemed outdated and discredited raised the spectre of other European nations adopting a similar orientation.

According to the *Oxford English Dictionary*, in the political meaning of the term, illiberal refers to 'one who is not liberal in opinions, etc.; one who is opposed to liberalism in politics'. This definition captures the outlook communicated by Orbán's version of illiberal democracy. However, the term 'illiberal' also conveys another meaning, which pertains to attitudes towards the views and freedoms of others. In this sense, the *Oxford English Dictionary* defines illiberal as 'not generous in respect to the opinions, rights, or liberty of others; narrow-minded, bigoted'. Illiberalism in this sense often characterizes the attitude and behaviour of those who otherwise take exception to the idea of illiberal democracy.

One of the most striking features of the cultural conflict between the two versions of illiberalism is that the critics of populism and of Hungarian conservative nationalism are simply not aware of their own illiberal attitudes and assumptions. One of the most unattractive features of such illiberal liberals is that they assume that they have the right to impose their attitudes and views on those who do not share them. This unpleasant and arrogant behaviour is now all too visible in universities in the Anglo-American world, where in some cases students are expected to attend seminars that train them to become aware of their bias and thus change their attitudes. In some American universities, students are expected to participate in diversity awareness classes and to adopt the values they promote, regardless of their previous inclinations. Such illiberal paternalistic behaviour is bad enough when it occurs within the confines of a university. It becomes far more insidious when it assumes the form of lecturing people in a different nation and society about what values they should live by. It becomes even worse when, as in the case of the dispute about European values, some of the supporters of the federalist project threaten a nation such as Hungary with the ultimatum – change your values or else!

There is more than a hint of cultural superiority about the tone adopted by Western critics of Hungary. Remarkably, their imperious attitude echoes colonialist practice of branding as exotic or inferior a whole people. James Traub, in his article 'Hungary's 500 Year-Old Victim Complex', reduces a whole nation to a psychologically illiterate and morally dissolute community. The language he uses not only displays ignorance of Hungary's history but a breathtaking insensitivity towards the historical challenges it faced. He contends that 'Hungarians share a collective pathology known as the "Trianon syndrome"'.[31] The sense of historical injustice and loss that many Hungarians feel towards Trianon is here recast into a psychological pathology. Through medicalizing Hungarian national attitudes, a whole people is pathologized and rendered morally inferior.

Speculation about Hungary's victim complex is integral to a political narrative that attributes this nation's cultural attitudes and opinions to qualities that are usually associated with the status of inferiority. One need not be a supporter of the Fidesz government to grasp that what is at work in this conflict is the project of rendering Hungarian cultural attitudes inferior to those of its critics. As Agnes Gagyi concludes, the language of 'superiority/inferiority' has even been internalized by domestic opponents of Fidesz, whose 'discourse were addressed in the sharpest language of essentialized inferiority'. What is astonishing about the language adopted by critics of 'Hungarian racism' is the 'terminology of human inferiority' they developed in addressing "Hungarians"'.[32]

According to the critics of Hungary's collective pathology, one of the main symptoms of this disease is this nation's reluctance to celebrate the value of diversity. This point was frequently reiterated during the heated exchanges that surrounded the Hungarian government's refusal to abide by the EU's migration policy in 2015. At the time Hungary was not merely condemned for closing its borders to migrants but also for not signing up to the values of diversity and multiculturalism. In effect, what was at issue was that Hungary chose to remain a 'monoethnic' society. In his journey to Budapest, James Traub was surprised to discover that even opponents of the Hungarian government were less than enthusiastic about the project of turning the nation into a multicultural society. Traub reported:

> Like much of Eastern Europe, Hungary is a monoethnic society. Only 1.5 percent of Hungary's population has foreign citizenship, and one-third of these people are ethnic Hungarians. Outside of tourist districts, you don't see black or Asian or Arab people on the streets of Budapest – not to mention in the rest of the country. That struck most people I spoke to as a precious asset to be preserved. Hungarians look at Germany and France and see what they call "parallel societies," where Turks or Algerians live in their own worlds, suspicious of their hosts and threatening to them. And those are rich countries; Hungary has a stagnant economy that cannot offer jobs to newcomers. Why would Hungary want immigrants who don't want to integrate or simply can't?[33]

Traub's verdict on Hungary's reluctance to follow Germany and France down the path of multiculturalism was to concede that it 'needs to be acknowledged that resistance to accepting and resettling refugees from Middle Eastern wars, at least in the monoethnic societies of Eastern Europe, is natural, logical, and inevitable'. Other critics are far less charitable on this point: they insist that Hungary needs to fall in line with the EU's regime of diversity whether it likes it or not.

Those who bemoan Hungary's reluctance to internalize the value and practice of diversity are typically selective about what kind of diversity they value. They are enthusiastic about promoting diversity within a national community. But they are not prepared to accept the right of different nations to pursue a different path on their approach to domestic diversity. Their celebration of diversity does not extend to welcoming diversity between the political cultures of different nations. In practice, for illiberal liberals the right of nations to self-determination has become an outdated credo.

Crisis of valuation

Writing in *The Washington Post*, Miklos Haraszti, the former Hungarian dissident and opponent of the Fidesz government, warned his American readers, 'I watched a populist leader rise in my country' and added that, 'that's why I'm genuinely worried about America'.[34] Describing Hungary as a 'populist autocracy', Haraszti warned that the election of Donald Trump threatened to drag America down the same illiberal democratic path. Haraszti, like numerous illiberal liberal commentators, uses the term 'populist' interchangeably with 'illiberal democracy'. Indeed, in the cosmopolitan vocabulary the word populist serves to describe morally inferior people, 'who are not like us'. Typically populism is portrayed as authoritarian, illiberal, anti-democratic, and even racist. 'How can we resist illiberal democracy and populism?' was the title at a conference for NGO activists devoted to discussing 'the growing trend toward illiberal democracy, autocracy, and populism' held in November 2016 at the Human Rights House in Belgrade.[35]

The current tendency to portray populism as autocratic, illiberal, and xenophobic is the outcome of a polemical exercise designed to cast opponents in the worst possible light. In the twenty-first century, the meaning of populism has been distorted through the tendency of its opponents to attribute a wide range of negative qualities to it. 'As it is being used today, "populism" is a term of abuse applied by establishment thinkers to people whose lives they have not troubled to understand,' argued the British philosopher John Gray.[36] This usage of populism is principally directed at the values that the targets of its polemics possess. The hostility of anti-populist thinkers and policymakers towards populism to a large measure reflects the conflict between their values and those that influence the everyday life of people. This tendency is particularly visible in the media, where anti-populist contributors are often unable to take seriously people whose values are opposed to its worldview.

Anti-populist commentators are particularly uncomfortable with openly and explicitly engaging with a nation's citizens. In place of relying on winning an argument with the people, they prefer to rely on handing over policy decision-making to experts. The EU, where democracy is carefully limited and rationed so that the technocrat and expert can have the final say, has turned this practice of technocratic governance into an art form. Though critical of contemporary populism, the political scientist Cas Mudde has recognized that it constitutes what he calls an 'illiberal democratic' response to 'undemocratic liberalism'. Mudde wrote that populism 'criticises the exclusion of important issues from the political agenda by the elites and calls for their repoliticisation'.[37]

Mudde is right to underline the aspiration of a so-called populist for a democratic voice. But what really provokes the fury of anti-populists is the challenge to their values that this movement represents. As the political theorist Margaret Canovan pointed out, unlike so-called social movements, populism does not merely challenge the holder of power but also 'elite values'. Therefore its hostility is also directed at 'opinion formers and the media'.[38] Often the challenge posed by populist movements to elite values is expressed through their reluctance to abandon customs and traditions that elites have discarded: sentiments described by the use of that confusing term 'nostalgia'. This point is exemplified in an article titled 'Europe's Dangerous Nostalgia' by Javier Solana, the former secretary general of NATO. Solana writes:

> The European Union has a dangerous case of nostalgia. Not only is a yearning for the 'good old days' – before the EU supposedly impinged on national sovereignty – fueling the rise of nationalist political parties; European leaders continue to try to apply yesterday's solutions to today's problems.[39]

Solana points his finger at Poland and Hungary, where 'nationalism and anti-EU sentiment have surged'.

It appears that nostalgia is 'dangerous' because it draws people towards gaining meaning from the values of the past – such as national sovereignty. From this standpoint, the very search for meaning in tradition is likely to encourage opposition to the value system of the anti-populist defenders of the cultural *status quo*.

Many of the reactions and attitudes associated with populism constitute what Hannah Arendt would have characterized as the search for pre-political authority. The common quest for gaining meaning by forging pre-political solidarity can often express itself in affirming traditional family and community life and religion and solidarity. The attempt to reappropriate the moral goes directly against the grain of contemporary cosmopolitan thought and practice. In a sense, the tension between anti-populist illiberal liberalism and Hungary's illiberal democracy can be interpreted as a symptom of a *crisis of valuation*.

The concept of a crisis of valuation and the difficulty that liberal thought had with the domain of values was directly raised and discussed in the middle of the Second World War, by Károly Mannheim. In his wartime essays, Mannheim blamed liberal democracy's reluctance to engage with the realm of moral values for its political indecisiveness and defensiveness. The central point that he sought to convey was that society needed to believe in something tangible and that democracy had to come up with some convincing answers regarding the values that people should live by. He asserted that the simple affirmation of laissez-faire liberalism lacked the cultural depth necessary to inspire the public, and he sought an ethos that 'will differ from the relativist *laissez faire* of the previous age' and 'will have the courage to agree on some basic values which are acceptable to everybody who shares the traditions of Western civilization'.[40] Mannheim was far from clear about the constitution of these values, although his reference to values 'inherited from classical antiquity and even more from Christianity' showed a disposition towards the reappropriation of the legacy of Western civilization.

Mannheim's preoccupation with what he characterized as 'the crisis of valuation' anticipated some of the issues that surround the disputes over cultural values in Europe. The corrosive effects of the absence of consensus on basic values disturbed him. He wrote that 'there is nothing in our lives, not even on the level of basic habits such as food, manners, behaviour, about which our views are not at variance'; he observed that there is not even any agreement as to 'whether this great variety of opinions is good or bad, whether the greater conformity of the past or the modern emphasis on choice is to be preferred'. Nevertheless, Mannheim was certain that it is 'definitely not good to live in a society whose norms are unsettled and develop in an unsteady way'. The conclusion he drew from his assessment of the crisis of valuation was that 'the first step to be taken by democracies in contrast to their previous laissez-faire policy will consist in giving up their disinterest in valuations'.[41]

The problems raised by Mannheim over 70 years ago have rarely been directly confronted. Instead they have been evaded to the point that even some of the values that Mannheim could take for granted in the 1940s have become an object of dispute. Mannheim could still assume that his audience embraced 'the traditions of Western civilization' and looked upon it as a legacy to be passed on to future generations. That can no longer be assumed today.

As we noted in the previous chapters, twenty-first-century Western society has become ambivalent and even alienated from its civilizational legacy. And as far as its cultural elites are concerned, the very attempt to uphold that legacy constitutes a dangerous form of irrational populism. Such a stance serves as a form of self-justification that absolves anti-populist elites from the responsibility of having to engage and discuss with people who are not like them. There is no dialogue or communication between the anti-populist and the populist, which is why the current polarization between antithetical values is so dangerous.

Notes

1 Kende is cited in Harms (2015) pp. 349–350.
2 Cited in Harms (2015) pp. 350–351.
3 Lendvai (2012) p. 117.
4 Wilkin (2016) p. 83.
5 Gagyi (2016) p. 359.
6 Fromm, E. (1965) (originally published 1941) *Escape From Freedom*, Henry Holt and Company : NewYork, p. 3.
7 Cited in Fromm (1965) p. 3.
8 Cited in Borch (2012) p. 175.
9 Cited in Enyedi, Z. (2015). Plebeians, citoyens and aristocrats or where is the bottom of bottom-up? The case of Hungary. European populism in the shadow of the great recession. Studies in European political science, p. 342.
10 Habermas, J. (2011) 'Europe's Post-Democracy Era', *The Guardian*, 10 November 2011.
11 Scheppele, K. L. (2001) 'Democracy by Judiciary (Or Why the Courts Can Sometimes Be More Democratic Than Parliaments)', *University*, 1–3 November 2001, https://law.wustl.edu/harris/conferences/constitutionalconf/ScheppelePaper.pdf.
12 Solyom (2013) p. 135.
13 See the discussion in Boulanger (2006).
14 Pokol (2003) p. 82.

15 Scheppele, K.L. (2000) 'The Constitutional Basis of Hungarian Conservatism', Eastern European Constitutional Review, Vol 9, No 4, p. 16.
16 Scheppele (2000) p. 33.
17 Scheppele (2001) p. 56.
18 Müller, J.-W. (2013) *Safeguarding Democracy Inside the EU Brussels and the Future of Liberal Order*, Transatlantic Academy Paper Series, p. 12.
19 Müller (2013) p. 13.
20 www.opendemocracy.net/ourkingdom/anthony-barnett/debate-death-penalty-%E2% 80%93-and-then-move-on-to-rule-of-law.
21 Cited in Heartfield (2012) p. 56.
22 Traub, J. (2016) 'Liberalism Isn't Working', *Foreign Policy*, 7 July 2016.
23 Cited in Lyman, R. & Berendt, J. (2016) 'Obama Rebukes Poland's Right Wing Government', *The New York Times*, 8 July 2016.
24 Traub, J. (2016) 'It's Time for the Elites to Rise Up against the Ignorant Masses', *Foreign Policy*, 28 June 2016.
25 *ibid.*
26 Holmes (1993) Harvard., p. 3.
27 Holmes (1993) p. 4.
28 For a discussion of these trends in higher education- see Furedi (2016).
29 Hörcher (2011). The National Avowal. Politeja-Pismo Wydzialu Studiow Miedzynarodowych i Politycznych Uniwersytetu Jagiellonskiego, vol. 17, p. 19.
30 Full text of Viktor Orbán's speech at Băile Tuşnad (Tusnádfürdő) of 26 July 2014, http:// budapestbeacon.com/public-policy/full-text-of-viktor-orbans-speech-at-baile-tusnad-tusnadfurdo-of-26-july-2014/10592.
31 See Traub, J. 'Hungary's 500-Year-Old Victim Complex', *FP*, 28 October 2015.
32 Gagyi (2016) p. 359.
33 Traub, J. (2015) 'The Fearmonger of Budapest', *Foreign Policy*, 27 October 2015, https:// foreignpolicy.com/2015/10/27/the-fearmonger-of-budapest-orban-hungary-refugees-migrants-europe/.
34 Haraszti, M. (2016) 'I Watched a Populist Leader Rise in My country', *The Washington Post*, 28 December 2016.
35 http://humanrightshouse.org/Articles/22051.html.
36 Gray, J. (2016) 'The Strange Death of Liberal Politics', *New Statesman*, 5 July 2016.
37 Mudde, C. (2015) 'The Problem With Populism', *The Guardian*, 17 February 2015, www. theguardian.com/commentisfree/2015/feb/17/problem-populism-syriza-podemos-dark-side-europe.
38 Canovan, M. (1999) 'Trust the People! Populism and the Two Faces of Democracy', *Political studies*, vol. 47, no. 1, pp. 2–16.
39 Solana, J. (2016) 'Europe's Dangerous Nostalgia', *Project Syndicate*, 27 April 2016, www. socialeurope.eu/2016/04/europes-dangerous-nostalgia/.
40 Mannheim (1943) p. 7.
41 Mannheim (1943) p. 26.

CONCLUSION

The questions raised by Mannheim in his discussion of the crisis of valuation were rarely explored during the decades following the Second World War. The climate of ideological polarization during the early years of the Cold War made it relatively easy to avoid engaging with the unresolved problem of values, but from the 1950s onwards, the status of traditional values and the constitution of moral authority became a frequent subject of discussion. In Western societies, those who affirmed traditional values as sacred were directly challenged by modernizers who sought to promote the superior insights of science and expertise as the foundation of authority. By the 1960s and 1970s this conflict mutated into a veritable Culture War where tradition was increasingly forced on the defensive.[1]

Tradition and the knowledge that emerges through change have always existed in an uneasy relationship with one another. The tension between tradition and new values was already evident in Athens during fifth century BC, where the relationship between *doxa* (belief and opinion) and *episteme* (newly found knowledge) became a focus for debate.[2] Although societies such as Rome and Medieval Europe had a greater reverence for the traditions of the past than the Greeks, their uneasy relationship with changing knowledge has been a constant theme in human history.

In modern times, and especially during the post-Second World War era, the tension between the authority of tradition and other forms of legitimation, such as science, expertise, or the rule of law, have deepened. Consequently, traditional cultural symbols of meaning and customs have lost much of their commanding force. However their moral authority, and the web of meaning they provided to communities, has not been replaced by a comparable alternative system of non-traditional values. The Culture Wars that followed the 1960s have been far more effective in undermining tradition than in constructing a substitute focus for the constitution of moral authority.

During the 1960s, the crisis of valuation that Mannheim discussed re-emerged in a purer cultural form. Despite its economic prosperity and considerable technological achievements, Western societies appeared to lack the moral resources with which to legitimate their way of life. Consequently, authority in all of its different dimensions was exposed to contestation.[3] The most striking manifestation of the moral crisis of the West was that it was not simply one form of authority that was put to question, but the *authority of authority*. Already, back in the 1950s, Hannah Arendt claimed that authority had become 'almost a lost cause'. In an essay that self-consciously referred to authority in the past tense – titled 'What Was Authority?' – Arendt insisted that 'authority has vanished from the modern world, and that if we raise the question what authority is, we can no longer fall back upon authentic and undisputable experiences common to all'.[4] Arendt's narrative of loss left little room for retaining illusions that authority in its classical form could survive. She drew attention to a dramatic development in the 'gradual breakdown' of 'the authority of parents over children, of teachers over pupils and, generally of the elders over the young',[5] and observed that this is 'the one form of authority' that existed in 'all historically known societies', as it is 'required as much by natural needs, the helplessness of the child, as by political necessity'. However, 'ours is the first century in which this argument no longer carries an overwhelming weight of plausibility and it announced its anti-authoritarian spirit more radically when it promised the emancipation of youth as an oppressed class and called itself the "century of the child"'. Arendt was less interested in the implosion of generational authority itself as she was in the extent to which it signified 'to what extremes the general decline of authority could go, even to the neglect of obvious natural necessities'.[6]

At the time, Arendt's lament about the 'lost cause' of authority did not provoke much response, and in the decades to follow, concern with the question of moral authority was confined to a relatively small group of mainly conservative intellectuals and commentators. One of the clearest responses to the narrative of loss of cultural authority was that of the conservative sociologist Robert Nisbet, who warned that the 'revolt against authority has already reached a higher point than in any other period in the West since perhaps the final years of the Roman Empire'.[7]

The devaluation of the moral status of the people

The response of the cultural elites of Western societies to the problems outlined by Arendt was to avoid an explicit engagement with the question of authority. Instead, the problem was sublimated into a concern about the moral status of the people and, in particular, those people who insisted on holding onto their traditions and refused to abide by the wisdom of the emerging class of non-traditional experts. This anti-populist ethos emerged a long time before the ascent of the post-Cold War populist movement.

The sublimation of the concern about the fragile state of authority into a preoccupation with the reliability of the public was connected to the widespread revulsion against authoritarianism that swept the West in the 1940s. In the immediate aftermath of the Second World War, the loathing against Nazism tended to intensify the sentiments of suspicion and hostility towards authority. This reaction fostered a climate of estrangement from authority, which was frequently interpreted as merely a milder version of authoritarianism. In this historical context, the practice of obedience was itself called into question and often associated with a negative and potentially pathological form of behaviour. The image of an obedient public unthinkingly following the orders of a demagogic Führer haunted the thinking of anti-populist thinkers.

In the immediate post-war period, concern about the reliability of the *demos* was frequently expressed through antipathy towards mass culture and the emotions it fostered. The emotional deficits of the people were depicted as one of the forces responsible for the scourge of authoritarian dictatorships. Reflections on the problem of authoritarianism frequently took the form of deprecating the capacity of the *demos* for informed consent. In 1950, the argument put forward by radical social critic Theodor Adorno that people inevitably defer to authorities that act against their interest, resonated with the anti-authoritarian temper of the times. Adorno observed that 'throughout the ages', since the oligarchy arose in Greece, 'the majority of the people frequently act blindly in accordance with the will of powerful institutions or demagogic figures, and in opposition both to the basic concepts of democratism and their own rational interest'.[8]

Adorno was right to link his classical disdain for the people to the Greek elite's contempt towards populism. Anti-populist political theory developed in Athens in response to the failure of the oligarchy to assert its authority over the people. Athens was a community where authority was invested in the people and the opinions they expressed through the Athenian assembly and other public venues. The legitimacy enjoyed by public opinion and its democratic culture was reinforced by historical events such as the defeat of the Persians by the Athenian navy at the battle of Salamis: it was the poor sailors of the navy rather than heroic upper-class warriors who were identified with the glory of Athens. According to one account, the victory at Salamis 'helped open the public arena in both size and substance beyond anything known in the Hellenic world by legitimating the claims to power and authority of the poor whose courage and steadfastness had won the victory'.[9]

Athens provides an early example of the authorization of popular sovereignty. In fifth century BC, Plato's Socrates provided one of the earliest critiques of populism. He regarded the authority of public opinion as far too wedded to custom and tradition; he was preoccupied by the authority enjoyed by the *demos* and concerned by the insufficiency of its opinion to point the way to the truth. In some of the comments attributed to him in the *Apology*, what he seeks is not opinion but 'opinions that are better informed and more completely thought through'.[10] Socrates argued that society was ready to defer to the views of experts and ignore the opinion of ordinary folk on technical matters such as shipbuilding and architecture, and he was at a loss as to why the same approach was not adopted in relation to political life. In his dialogue with Protagoras, Socrates states that 'when it is something to do with the government of the country that is to be debated, the man who gets up to advise them may be a builder or equally well a blacksmith or a shoemaker, a merchant or ship owner, rich or poor, of good family or none'.[11] As far as he is concerned, 'what most people think' on political matters is far less important than the views of the one man who really understands the issues at stake – the expert.[12] That Adorno echoed his views more than two thousand years later illustrates the enduring tension between an expert-directed polity and one based on popular sovereignty.

Plato's disdain for the *demos* and his advocacy of the authority of the expert reappears in a modern form in anti-populist cultural script. So it is not surprising that during the EU Referendum campaign in Britain in June 2016, anti-populist commentators reacted with outrage to the statement made by the conservative cabinet minister Michael Gove, that 'I think the people of this country have had enough of experts'. The palpable sense of horror with which the anti-populist media responded to this statement indicated that from its standpoint, the authority of the expert stood between civilization and the dreaded populist masses.

If not the expert, then who will exercise authority over the *demos*? This was a question that was formulated a long time before the emergence of the current anti-populist cultural script. The conviction that the people are morally and intellectually inferior to their enlightened superiors constitutes the historical foundation of the anti-populist imagination. Historically, this sentiment tended to be associated with the oligarchical defenders of the prevailing social hierarchy. In recent decades, such sentiments pervade the language of illiberal liberalism. Anti-populist commentators are convinced that the *demos* is a) rarely capable of grasping its own interest and b) easily swayed through the manipulation of its irrational emotions by the simplistic arguments of populist politicians. 'Do you feel like you live in a nation of idiots?' asked the consummate cynic Michael Moore, knowing that his very educated American readers will share his contempt for his moral inferiors.[13]

Back in the early 1990s, the American cultural theorist Christopher Lasch drew attention to the growing grudge that the illiberal liberal elites appeared to bear towards populism. He observed that, whereas 'formerly liberals had worried about the decline of popular participation in politics', now 'they began to wonder whether "apathy" might not be a blessing in disguise'.[14] Since the 1990s the anti-populist sentiments that Lasch identified have hardened into a rigid ideology that is directed towards de-legitimating the customs and attitudes of ordinary people. Many of the themes explored earlier – the distancing of people from the past, the decoupling of nationality from the state, the cultural war against tradition – are integral to a wider project of re-educating people through calling into question the values into which they were socialized.

It is ironic that anti-populist commentators claim to be outraged by Orbán's idea of illiberal democracy, when they themselves adopt such profoundly illiberal attitudes towards the practice of democracy of the people. The outlook of anti-populism feeds on a diet of negative values. It continually deploys the politics of fear and uses warnings about the threat posed by populism to influence public life. Despite its advocacy of transnational institutions and cosmopolitan values, the current ideology of anti-populism is ultimately far more parochial than the targets of its critique. Its focus is on group rights and, in the context of the EU, it is devoted to gaining privileges for them. Illiberal liberalism has lost sight of the need to affirm the common good and prefers to deal with members of different identity groups rather than with individual citizens. The individual citizen, who has been central to the politics of classical liberalism, has been displaced by the interests of the group.

Given the influence of anti-populist culture in Western institutions and the media, its profoundly anti-democratic sensibility is rarely commented upon. Indeed anti-populist critics of illiberal-minded political movements and politicians rarely recognize their own problem with liberalism. For example, anti-populist writers claim that the conception of the people put forward by populist politicians strongly resembles that of the German right-wing legal theorist Carl Schmitt. Schmitt's authoritarian political theory appealed to many intellectual supporters of the Nazi Party and remains attractive to sections of the twenty-first-century far right; however, his polemic against liberalism bears an uncanny resemblance to the rhetoric that contemporary anti-populists adopt towards their opponents. In his most influential book, *The Concept of the Political*, Schmitt argued that all true politics were ultimately founded on the distinction between friend and enemy. His highly polarized friend-enemy distinction left no space for the kind of dialogue and debate that is associated with an open democratic society. Unfortunately, anti-populist politicians and thinkers have unthinkingly adopted the friend-enemy conception of the political, and they frequently communicate this disturbing attitude towards public life.

The battle lines between friend and enemy were unambiguously drawn by Hillary Clinton during the 2016 American presidential elections when she notoriously referred to supporters of Donald Trump as a 'basket of deplorables'. That they were not to be regarded as simply misguided political opponents but as the enemy was spelled out by the headline of a comment piece in *The Washington Post:* 'Trump can't just be defeated. He must be humiliated'.[15] Schmitt would certainly have approved the title of an article by Dean Obeidallah in the *Daily Beast:* 'Donald Trump Can't Merely Be Defeated- He and His Deplorables Must Be Crushed'[16]

The Schmittian friend-enemy distinction has become far too influential in the framing of the conflict over values in Europe. There are far too few voices who are prepared to uphold a genuinely liberal orientation in public life, even in the heat of the conflict. Yet the stakes are high, and it is likely that if anything, the conflict over values will acquire an even greater force in the years ahead.

The clash between the EU oligarchy and Hungary has touched on a variety of issues. But the most fundamental difference between the two sides is their contrasting positions on the status of national sovereignty. Table 1 outlines the key points of difference between the two sides in Europe's Culture War.

The main reason why the question of national sovereignty has become so important in the current cultural conflict in Europe is because it is in the context of a national community that most people gain meaning and develop their identity. That

TABLE 1 Competing cultural values

Uphold tradition	Post-traditional
Historical continuity	Year Zero history
National culture and sovereignty	Denationalized identity
Attachment to nation state	Attachment to transnational institutions
Community	Diversity
Popular sovereignty	Authority of the expert

is why the debate on migration and borders in Europe is not simply a dispute about immigration; it is about a much wider existential question of 'who am I and where do I stand in this world?'

The casual attitude that the EU appears to adopt towards borders is founded upon its hostility to the principle of national sovereignty. As we noted, it regards loyalty to the nation as a marker for populism and prefers people to adopt attachments either to transnational institutions or to sub-national minority causes. Yet borders, which are essential for the maintenance of national sovereignty, are so far the only foundation that humanity has discovered for the institutionalization of democratic accountability. It is within familiar borders that citizens felt confident to work out their ideas and enter into dialogue and debate with one another. Without borders a citizen becomes a subject to a power that cannot be held to account: and this is why – from a democratic perspective – it is so important to counter the anti-populist crusade against national sovereignty.

The experience of history indicates that popular sovereignty and the values associated with its exercise is the most robust foundation on which public life can flourish. Fukuyama argued that there is 'no universal principle of legitimacy other than the sovereignty of the people'.[17] Unfortunately this principle remains constantly challenged by anti-populist opinion, which has no trust in the capacity of the people to make intelligent choices. Illiberal anti-populism constitutes the principal threat to democracy in Europe today.

Notes

1 For a discussion of this chapter of the Culture Wars, see Furedi (2014) Chapter 6.
2 See Saxonhouse (2008) p. 38 on this discussion.
3 This point is developed in chapter 16 of Furedi (2013).
4 Arendt (2006) p. 81.
5 Arendt (1956) p. 403.
6 Arendt (1956) p. 404.
7 Nisbet (1972) pp. 3, 4, 12.
8 Adorno (1950) p. 418.
9 Euben (1997) p. 65.
10 Euben (1997) p. 107.

11 Protagoras 319b-d.
12 See *Crito* (47b10–11).
13 Moore (2001) p. 87.
14 Lasch (1991) p. 153.
15 See www.washingtonpost.com/opinions/trump-cant-just-be-defeated-he-must-be-humiliated/2016/10/21/d03ed0e0-9792-11e6-bb29-bf2701dbe0a3_story.html?utm_term=.5741c8157c22.
16 www.thedailybeast.com/articles/2016/11/02/donald-trump-can-t-merely-be-defeated-he-and-his-deplorables-must-be-crushed.html.
17 Fukuyama (1992) p. 45.

BIBLIOGRAPHY

Abts, K. & Rummens, S. (2007) 'Populism versus Democracy', *Political Studies*, vol. 55, no.2.

Adorno, T.W. (1950) 'Democratic Leadership and Mass Manipulation', in Gouldner, A. (ed), *Studies in Leadership: Leadership and Democratic Action*, Harper & Brothers: New York.

Arendt, H. (1951) *The Origins of Totalitarianism*, Harcourt Brace Jovanovich: New York.

Arendt, H. (1956) 'Authority in the Twentieth Century', *The Review of Politics*, vol. 18, no.4.

Arendt, H. (2006) 'What Is Authority', in Arendt, H. (ed), *Between Past and Future*, Penguin Books: London.

Auer, S. (2010) 'New Europe: Between Cosmopolitan Dreams and Nationalist Nightmares', *JCMS: Journal of Common Market Studies*, vol. 48, no.5.

Baumeister, A. (2007) 'Diversity and Unity the Problem with Constitutional Patriotism', *European Journal of Political Theory*, vol. 6, no.4.

Beck, U. (2005) *Power in the Global Age: A New Global Political Economy*, Polity Press: Cambridge.

Beck, U. & Grande, E. (2007) *Cosmopolitan Europe*, Polity Press: Cambridge.

Beetham, D. (1991a) 'Max Weber and the Legitimacy of the Modern State', *Analyse & Kritik*, nos.34–35.

Beetham, D. (1991b) *The Legitimation of Power*, Macmillan: Houndmills, Basingstoke.

Behr, H. (2007) 'The European Union in the Legacies of Imperial Rule? EU Accession Politics Viewed from a Historical Comparative Perspective', *European Journal of International Relations*, vol. 13, no.2.

Bendix, R. (1978) *Kings or People: Power and the Mandate to Rule*, University of California Press: Berkeley.

Berend, T.I. (ed) (1986) *Helyünk Európába; Nézetek és koncpeciok a 20 századi Magyarországon*, vol. 2, Magvető Kiadó: Budapest.

Berger, S. (2007) 'Writing National Histories in Europe: Reflections on the Pasts, Presents, and Futures of a tradition', in Jarausch, K.H. & Lindenberger, T. (eds), *Conflicted Memories: Europeanizing Contemporary Histories*, Berghahn Books: Oxford.

Berman, H. (1983) *Law and Revolution: The Formation of the Western Legal Tradition*, Harvard University Press: Cambridge, MA.

Bibo, I. (1976) *The Paralysis of International Institutions and the Remedies: A Study of Self-Determination, Concord among the Major Powers and Political Arbitration*, The Harvester Press: Sussex.

Bideleux, R. (2015) 'The "Orientalization" and "de-Orientalization" of East Central Europe and the Balkan Peninsula', *Journal of Contemporary Central and Eastern Europe*, vol. 23, no. 1.

Black, D. (2011) *Moral Time*, Oxford University Press: New York.

Borch, C. (2012) *The Politics of Crowds: An Alternative History of Sociology*, Cambridge University Press: Cambridge.

Borsody, S. (1988) 'Preface', in Borsody, S. (ed), *The Hungarians: A Divided Nation*, Yale Press: New Haven.

Boulanger, C. (2006) *Europeanization through Judicial Activism? The Hungarian Constitutional Court's Legitimacy and the "Return to Europe"*, Springer: Netherlands.

Brenan, J. (2016) *Against Democracy*, Princeton University Press: Princeton.

Bristow, J. (2015) *Baby Boomers and Generational Conflict*, Palgrave: Houndsmills, Basingstoke.

Calliagro, O. (2013) *Negotiating Europe: The EU Promotion of Europeanness since the 1950s*, Palgrave Macmillan: Basingstoke.

Calliagro, O. (2015) 'Legitimation through Remembrance? The Changing Regimes of Historicity of European Integration', *Journal of Contemporary European Studies*, vol. 23, no. 3, pp. 330–343.

Canovan, M. (1999) 'Trust the People! Populism and the Two Faces of Democracy', *Political Studies*, vol. 47, no. 1, pp. 2–16.

Closa, C. (2011) 'Negotiating the Past: Claims for Recognition and Policies of Memory in the EU', *Institute of Public Goods and Policies (IPP) Working Paper* 08.

Cvijic, S. & Zucca, L. (2004) 'Does The European Constitution Need Christian Values', *Oxford Journal of Legal Studies*, vol. 24, no. 4.

Delanty, G. (1996) 'Habermas and Post-National Identity: Theoretical Perspectives on the Conflict in Northern Ireland', *Irish Political Studies*, vol. 11, no. 1.

Della Sala, V. (2010) 'Political Myth, Mythology and the European Union', *Journal of Common Market Studies*, vol. 48, no. 1, p. 3.

Della Sala, V. (2016) 'Europe's Odyssey?: Political Myth and the European Union', *Nations and Nationalism*, vol. 22, no. 3.

Deme, L. (1998) 'Perceptions and Problems of Hungarian Nationality and National Identity in the Early 1990s', *International Journal of Politics, Culture and Society*, vol. 12, no. 2, pp. 309–310.

Deutsch, K.W. (1969) *Nationalism and Its Alternatives*, Alfred Knopf: New York.

Dromi, S. & Illouz, E. (2010) 'Recovering Morality, Pragmatic Sociology and Literary Studies', *New Literary History*, vol. 41, no. 2, pp. 351–369.

Egeddy, G. (2013) 'Conservatism and Nation-Models in Hungary', *Hungarian Review*, vol. 7, no. 6.

Eley, G. (1988) 'Nazism, Politics and the Images of the Past: Thoughts on the West German Historikerstreit, 1986–1987', *Past and Present*, no. 121.

Enyedi, Z. (2015) 'Plebeians, Citoyens and Aristocrats or Where Is the Bottom of Bottom-Up? The Case of Hungary', *European Populism in the Shadow of the Great Recession: Studies in European Political Science*, pp. 235–250.

Euben, J.P. (1997) *Corrupting Youth; Political Education, Democratic Culture, and Political Theory*, Princeton University Press: Princeton.

Evans, R.J.W. (2003) 'Hungarian Nationalism in International Context', *The Historian*, vol. 77, Spring.

Foret, F. & Littoz-Monnet, A. (2014) 'Legitimisation and Regulation of and through Values', *Politique européenne*, no. 45.

Fowler, B. (2004) 'Nation, State, Europe and National Revival in Hungarian Party Politics: The Case of the Millennial Commemorations', *Europe-Asia Studies*, vol. 56, no. 1.

Friedman, L. (1994) *The Republic of Choice, Law, Authority and Culture*, Harvard University Press: Cambridge, MA.

Friedrich, C.J. (1972) *Tradition and Authority*, The Pall Mall Press: London.

Fromm, E. (1969) (originally published 1941) *Escape From Freedom*, Henry Holt and Company: New York.

Fukuyama, F. (1992) *The End of History and the Last Man*, The Free Press: New York.

Furedi, F. (2013) *Authority: A Sociological History*, Cambridge University Press: Cambridge.

Furedi, F. (2014) *First World War: Still No End in Sight*, Bloomsbury: London.

Furedi, F. (2016) *What's Happened to the University: A Sociological Exploration of Its Infantilisation*, Routledge: London.

Gagyi, A. (2016) '"Coloniality of Power" in East Central Europe: External Penetration as Internal Force in Post-Socialist Hungarian Politics', *Journal of World-Systems Research*, vol. 22, no. 2.

Geehr, R.S. (1990) *Karl Lueger: Mayor of fin de siècle Vienna*, Wayne State University Press: Detroit, MI.

Grafstein, R. (1981) 'The Failure of Weber's Conception of Legitimacy: Its Causes and Implications', *The Journal of Politics*, vol. 43, no. 2.

Haas, E. (1958) *The Unity of Europe: Political, Social and Economic Forces, 1950–57*, Stanford University Press: Stanford.

Habermas, J. (1988) 'Historical Consciousness and Post-Traditional Identity: Remarks on the Federal Republic's Orientation to the West', *Acta Sociologica*, vol. 31, no. 1, pp. 3–13.

Habermas, J. (2016) *The Crisis of the European Union*, Polity: Cambridge.

Harms, V. (2015) *Destined or Doomed? Hungarian Dissidents and Their Western Friends, 1973–1998*. Diss. University of Pittsburgh.

Hayes, C.J.H. (1960) (originally published in 1926) *Nationalism as a Religion*, Macmillan: New York.

Heartfield, J. (2012) *The European Union and the End of Politics*, Zero Books: London.

Herz, F. (1951) (originally published in 1944) *Nationality in History and Politics*, Routledge & Kegan Paul: London.

Hobsbawm, E. (2004) *The Age of Extremes: The Short Twentieth Century, 1914–1991*, Abacus Books: London.

Hobson, J. (1988) *Imperialism: A Study*, Unwin Hyman: London.

Holmes, S. (1993) *The Anatomy of Antiliberalism*, Harvard University Press: Cambridge, MA.

Hörcher (2011). The National Avowal. *Politeja-Pismo Wydzialu Studiow Miedzynarodowych i Politycznych Uniwersytetu Jagiellonskiego*, vol. 17,

Hörcher, F. (2014) 'Communal Values in the New Hungarian Fundamental Law: The Habermas-Ratzinger Debate and the Use of the Humanities in Constitutional Interpretation', in *Verfassunggebung in Konsolidierten Demokratien* (pp. 346–365). Nomos Verlagsgesellschaft mbH & Co. KG.

Huxley, J. (1950) 'New Bottles for New Wine: Ideology and Scientific Knowledge', *The Journal of the Royal Anthropological Institute of Great Britain and Ireland*, vol. 80, nos. 1–2, pp. 7–23.

Jaume, L. (2010) 'Citizen and State Under the French Revolution', in Hanley, R.P. & McMahon, D.M. (eds), *The Enlightenment: Critical Concepts in Historical Studies*, vol. 5, Routledge: London.

Jeszenszky, G. (1989) 'The Hungarian Reception of "Soctus Viator"', *Hungarian Studies*, vol. 5/2.

Kaiser, W. (2015) 'Clash of Cultures: Two Milieus in the European Union's: A New Narrative for Europe', *Project, Journal of Contemporary European Studies*, vol. 23, no. 3, pp. 364–377.

Kaltwasser, C. R. (2014) 'The Responses of Populism to Dahl's Democratic Dilemmas', *Political Studies*, vol. 62, no. 3, pp. 470–487.

Karlsson, K.-G. (2010) 'The Uses of History and the Third Wave of Europeanisation', in Pakier, M., & Stråth, B. (eds), *A European Memory? Contested Histories and Politics of Remembrance*, Berghahn Books: New York.

Kautsy, K. (1925) *Foundations of Christianity: A Study in Christian Origin*, George Allen & Unwin: London.

Kecskés, G. (2015) 'Egy befolyásszerzési kísérlet anatómiája. Franciaország Kelet-Közép-Európa-politikája az 1920-as években', *KÜLÜGYI SZEMLE*, vol. 4.

Kis, J. (2000) 'Nation Building and Beyond', *Habitus*, no.2.

Klinke, I. (2014) 'European Integration Studies and the European Union's Eastern Gaze', *Millennium Journal of International Studies*, vol. 43, no.2, pp. 567–583.

Kohn, H. (1946) *The Idea of Nationalism*, Macmillan: New York.

Kokut, U. (2012) *Liberalization Challenges in Hungary: Elitism, Progressivism, and Populism*, Palgrave: London.

Konrad, G. (1984) *Antipolitics: An Essay*, Harcourt Brace Jovanovich, Publishers: San Diego.

Kovács, M. (2014) *Magyars and Political Discourses in the New Millennium: Changing Meanings in Hungary at the Start of the Twenty-First Century*, Lexington Books: Lanham, MD.

Krastev, I. (2007) 'The Strange Death of the Liberal Consensus', *Journal of Democracy*, vol. 18, no.4.

Laclau, E. (2007) *On Populist Reason*, Verso: London.

Larat, F. (2005) 'Presenting the Past: Political Narratives on European History and the Justification of EU Integration', *German Law Journal*, vol. 6, no.2.

Lasch, C. (1991) *The True and Only Heaven: Progress and Its Critics*, Norton: New York.

Lendvai, P. (2012) *Hungary: Between Democracy and Authoritarianism*, Hurst & Company: London.

Magyar Köztársoság Kulugyminiszterium as a Integrációs Stratégiai Munkacsoport (1998) *Magyarország a '90-es években: A Magyar kormany válasza az Europai Unió kérdöivére – rövidett változat*, Budapest.

Mälksoo, M. (2009) 'The Memory Politics of Becoming European: The East European Subalterns and the Collective Memory of Europe', *European Journal of International Relations*, vol. 15, no.4.

Mannheim, K. (1943) *Diagnosis of Our Time: Wartime Essays of a Sociologist*, Routledge & Kegan Paul Ltd: London.

Márai, S. (2000) *Memoir of Hungary 1944–1948*, Corvina: Budapest.

Martín-Arroyo, P. (2014) *'Histoeuropeanisation': Challenges and Implications of (Re)writing the History of Europe 'Europeanly', 1989–2015*, College of Europe Natolin Campus: Warszawa.

McDonald, M. (2005) 'EU Policy and Destiny: A Challenge for Anthropology Guest Editorial by Maryon McDonald', *Anthropology Today*, vol. 21, no.1.

Meier, C. (2005) *The Uses of History: From Athens to Auschwitz*, Harvard University Press: Harvard, MA.

Mikulova, K. (2013) '"Potemkin Europeanisation"? Dynamics of Party Competition in Poland and Hungary in 1998–2004', *East European Politics & Societies*, vol. 28, no.1, pp. 163–186.

Möhring, J. & Prins, G. (2013) 'Sail On, O Ship of State', in Möhring, J., & Prins, G. (2013) (eds.) *Sail On O Ship Of State,* Notting Hill Editions : London.

Moore, M. (2001) *Stupid White Men . . . and Other Sorry Excuses for the State of the Nation!*, Regan Books: New York.

Müller, J.-W. (2006) 'On the Origins of Constitutional Patriotism', *Contemporary Political Theory*, vol. 5, no.3, pp. 287–288.

Müller, J.-W. (2007) *Constitutional Patriotism*, Princeton University Press, Princeton.

Müller, J.-W. (2013) *Safeguarding Democracy Inside the EU Brussels and the Future of Liberal Order,* Transatlantic Academy Paper Series, p.19, http://www.transatlanticacademy.org/publications/safeguarding-democracy-inside-eu-brussels-and-future-liberal-order.

Müller, J.-W. (2014) 'The End of Christian Democracy', *Foreign Affairs*, July.

Müller, J.-W. (2016) 'Angela Merkel's Misunderstood Christian Mission', *Foreign Policy*, 18 March.

Müller, J.-W. (2016a) *What Is Populism*, University of Pennsylvania Press: Philadelphia.

Neumayer, L. (2015) 'Integrating the Central European Past into a Common Narrative: The Mobilizations Around the "Crimes of Communism" in the European Parliament', *Journal of Contemporary European Studies*, vol. 23, no.3.

Nicolson, H. (1965) *Peacemaking 1919*, Grosset & Dunlap: Boston.

Nisbet, R. (1972) 'The Nemesis of Authority', *The Intercollegiate Review*, Winter-Spring.

Örkény, A. (2005) 'Hungarian National Identity', *International Journal of Sociology*, vol. 35, no. 4, Winter.

Risso, L. (2009) 'Cracks in a Façade of Unity: The French and Italian Christian Democrats and the Launch of the European Integration Process, 1945–1957', *Religion, State & Society*, vol. 37, nos. 1–2.

Pänke, J. (2015) 'The Fallout of the EU's Normative Imperialism in the Eastern Neighborhood', *Problems of Post-Communism*, vol. 62, no. 6, pp. 350–363.

Peter, L. (2003) 'The Holy Crown of Hungary, Visible and Invisible', *SEER*, vol. 81, no. 3.

Plumb, J.H. (1989) *The Death of the Past*, Macmillan: London.

Pokol, B. (2003) 'Separation of Powers and Parliamentarism in Hungary', *East European Quarterly*, vol. 37, no. 1.

Prins, G. & Salisbury, R. (2008) *Risk, Threat and Security: The Case of the United Kingdom*, RUSI: London.

Rabinbach, A. (1988) 'The Jewish Question in the German Question', *New German Critique*, no. 44.

Risse, T. & Engelmann-Martin, D. (2002) 'Identity Politics and European Integration: The Case of Germany', in Pagden, A. (ed), *The Idea of Europe: From Antiquity to the European Union*, vol. 13, Cambridge University Press: Cambridge.

Rousso, H. (2016) *The Latest Catastrophe: History, the Present, the Contemporary*, The University of Chicago Press: Chicago.

Rowe, D. (2009) 'The Concept of the Moral Panic: An Historico-Sociological Positioning', in Lemmings, D., & Walker, C. (eds), *Moral Panics, the Media and the Law in Early Modern England*, Palgrave Macmillan: Houndmills, Basingstoke.

Saxonhouse, A.W. (2008) *Free Speech and Democracy in Ancient Athens*, Cambridge University Press: Cambridge.

Scheppele, K.L. (2000) 'The Constitutional Basis of Hungarian Conservatism', *Eastern European Constitutional Review*, vol. 9, no. 4, Spring.

Schmitt, K. (2007) *The Concept of the Political*, University of Chicago Press: Chicago.

Scruton, R. (2013) 'Introduction', in Möhring, J., & Prins, G. (2013) (eds.) *Sail On O Ship Of State*, Notting Hill Editions : London.

Sennett, R. (2001) *Authority*, Vintage Books : New York.

Seton-Watson, R. (1911) *The Southern Slav Question and the Habsburg Monarchy*, Constable & Co.: London.

Settele, C. (2015) 'Including Exclusion in European Memory? Politics of Remembrance at the House of European History', *Journal of Contemporary European Studies*, vol. 23, no. 3.

Sforza, C. (1943) 'Italy and Her Neighbours', *Foreign Affairs*, October.

Shore, C. (1999) 'Inventing Homo Europaeus: Cultural Politics of European Integration', *Ethnologia Europaea. Journal of European Ethnology*, vol. 29, no. 2.

Shore, C. (2000) *Building Europe: The Cultural Politics of European Integration*, Routledge: London.

Solyom, L. (2013) 'The Role of Constitutional Courts in the Transition to Democracy With Special Reference to Hungary', *International Sociology*, vol. 18, no. 1.

Spiro, H.J. (1958) 'Authority, Values, and Policy', in Friedrich, C.J. (ed), *Authority, Nomos 1*, Harvard University Press: Cambridge, MA.

Steed, H.W. (1913) *The Hapsburg Monarchy*, Constable: London.

Sugar, P. (2000) 'The More It Changes, the More Hungarian Nationalism Remains the Same', *Austrian History Yearbook*, vol. 31.

Szabó, M. (1991) 'A Kinos Forradalom', in Dénes, I. Z. (ed) (2008), *Liberalizmus És Nemzettudat*, Argumentum Kiadó: Budapest.

Szekfü, G. (1939) *Mi a Magyar?*, Magyar Szemle Társaság: Budapest.

Tartakoff, L.Y. (2012) 'Religion, Nationalism, History, and Politics in Hungary's New Constitution', *Society*, vol. 49.

Theiler, T. (2005) *Political Symbolism and European Integration*, Manchester University Press: Manchester.

Tonnies, F. (1955) *Community and Association*, Routledge & Kegan Paul Ltd: London.

Trencsényi, B. (2014) 'Beyond Liminality? The Kulturkampf of the Early 2000s in East Central Europe', *Boundary 2*, vol. 41, no.1.

Turner, B. (1992) *Max Weber: From History to Modernity*, Routledge: London.

Van Iterson, S. & Nenadović, M. (2013) 'The Danger of Not Facing History: Exploring the Link between Education about the Past and Present-Day Anti-Semitism and Racism in Hungary', *Intercultural Education*, vol. 24, nos.1–2.

Vardy, S.B. (1983) 'The Impact of Trianon Upon Hungary and the Hungarian Mind: The Nature of Interwar Hungarian Irredentism', *Hungarian Studies Review*, vol. 10, no.1, p. 4.

Weber, M. (1978) (edited by Roth, G. & Wittich, C.) *Economy and Society: An Outline of Interpretive Sociology*, vols. 1 & 2, University of California Press: Berkeley.

Wilkin, P. (2016) *Hungary's Crisis of Democracy: The Road to Serfdom*, Lexington Books: Lanham, MD.

Wodak, R. (2015) *The Politics of Fear What Right-Wing Populist Discourses Mean*, Sage: London.

INDEX

Page numbers in italics indicate figures and tables.